D1519643

▶ Professional Learning, Induction and Critical Reflection

DOI: 10.1057/9781137473028.0001

Other Palgrave Pivot titles

Graeme Kirkpatrick: The Formation of Gaming Culture: UK Gaming Magazines, 1981–1995

Candice C. Carter: Social Education for Peace: Foundations, Teaching, and Curriculum for Visionary Learning

Dilip K. Das: An Enquiry into the Asian Growth Model

Jan Pakulski and Bruce Tranter: The Decline of Political Leadership in Australia? Changing Recruitment and Careers of Federal Politicians

Christopher W. Hughes: Japan's Foreign and Security Policy under the 'Abe Doctrine': New Dynamism or New Dead End?

Eleanor Sandry: Robots and Communication

Hyunjung Lee: Performing the Nation in Global Korea: Transnational Theatre

Creso M. Sá and Andrew J. Kretz: The Entrepreneurship Movement and the University

Emma Bell: Soft Power and Freedom under the Coalition: State-Corporate Power and the Threat to Democracy

Ben Ross Schneider: Designing Industrial Policy in Latin America: Business-State Relations and the New Developmentalism

Tamer Thabet: Video Game Narrative and Criticism: Playing the Story

Raphael Sassower: Compromising the Ideals of Science

David A. Savage and Benno Torgler: The Times They Are A Changin': The Effect of Institutional Change on Cooperative Behaviour at 26,000 ft over Sixty Years

Mike Finn (editor): The Gove Legacy: Education in Britain after the Coalition

Clive D. Field: Britain's Last Religious Revival? Quantifying Belonging, Behaving, and Believing in the Long 1950s

Richard Rose and Caryn Peiffer: Paying Bribes for Public Services: A Global Guide to Grass-Roots Corruption

Altug Yalcintas: Creativity and Humour in Occupy Movements: Intellectual Disobedience in Turkey and Beyond

Joanna Black, Juan Carlos Castro, and Ching-Chiu Lin: Youth Practices in Digital Arts and New Media: Learning in Formal and Informal Settings

Wouter Peeters, Andries De Smet, Lisa Diependaele and Sigrid Sterckx: Climate Change and Individual Responsibility: Agency, Moral Disengagement and the Motivational Gap

Mark Stelzner: Economic Inequality and Policy Control in the United States

palgrave▸**pivot**

Professional Learning, Induction and Critical Reflection: Building Workforce Capacity in Education

Robyn Henderson
University of Southern Queensland, Australia

and

Karen Noble
University of Southern Queensland, Australia

palgrave
macmillan

DOI: 10.1057/9781137473028.0001

First published 2015 by
PALGRAVE MACMILLAN

Palgrave Macmillan in the UK is an imprint of Macmillan Publishers Limited, registered in England, company number 785998, of Houndmills, Basingstoke, Hampshire RG21 6XS.

Palgrave Macmillan in the US is a division of St Martin's Press LLC, 175 Fifth Avenue, New York, NY 10010.

Palgrave Macmillan is the global academic imprint of the above companies and has companies and representatives throughout the world.

Palgrave® and Macmillan® are registered trademarks in the United States, the United Kingdom, Europe and other countries.

ISBN: 978–1–137–47303–5 EPUB
ISBN: 978–1–137–47302–8 PDF
ISBN: 978–1–137–47301–1 Hardback

This book is printed on paper suitable for recycling and made from fully managed and sustained forest sources. Logging, pulping and manufacturing processes are expected to conform to the environmental regulations of the country of origin.

A catalogue record for this book is available from the British Library.

A catalog record for this book is available from the Library of Congress.

www.palgrave.com/pivot

DOI: 10.1057/9781137473028

For Karl and Allan, the most patient of men!

▶ *Serendipity brought us together and we are grateful for the friendship that we four now have. It gives 'us' the freedom to follow our passion for research and to work together without guilt, knowing you have each other for company, for pizza and movie nights, and the like.*

DOI: 10.1057/9781137473028.0001

Contents

DOI: 10.1057/9781137473028.0001

DOI: 10.1057/9781137473028.0001

Acknowledgements

We would like to thank:

▶ the students who taught us so much through accompanying us on the journey towards building a pedagogy of induction. Without their support, the research might not even have been imagined;

▶ all of the participants in the five teaching–learning projects that contributed to this book. The participants were University students, teachers, principals and other educators, doctoral students and academics;

▶ colleagues who bought into our vision and like us privileged the social as well as the academic: Ron Pauley, Marilyn Dorman, Jennifer Bundy, Henk Huijser, Anita Frederiks, Lindy Abawi, Michelle Turner and Linda De George-Walker;

▶ our co-collaborator from the windy city across the ocean: Judith A. Gouwens;

▶ program administrative teams who coordinated events: Beth McCormick, Debbie Blencowe, Anna Dean and Melanie Cameron;

▶ the multi-media team who helped our vision become a reality: Siân Carlyon, Jason Myatt, Jeff Black, Eddie Flemming, Greg Coombes, Jo Hallas, Ken Morton, Zoe Lynch, Sandra Adams and Ben Meares;

▶ research assistants: Helen Parker, Kimberley Schelberg and Jodie Gunders;

▶ University of Southern Queensland (USQ) and the support it offered through three Associate Fellowships.

DOI: 10.1057/9781137473028.0002

About the Authors

Robyn Henderson is an associate professor (literacies education) in the School of Teacher Education and Early Childhood at the University of Southern Queensland, Toowoomba, Australia. She researches in the fields of literacies education, family mobility and its effects on schooling, and the student learning journey in higher education. Themes related to pedagogies, diversity and capacity building run through her work. Robyn has published widely. She is the co-editor of four research books, the sole editor of another, and she is editor of the journal, *Literacy Learning: The Middle Years*.

Karen Noble is an associate professor and associate dean (teaching and learning) in the Faculty of Business, Education, Law and Arts at the University of Southern Queensland, Australia. Educational transitions and change, related to teaching and the education of teachers, is the focus of her academic work. Specifically, she is curious about the role of critical reflection and the impact of context on teacher professional learning and change. Working from a pedagogy of induction towards a culture of career support for teaching, she advocates for learning that is lifelong and life-wide and builds workforce capacity in education.

palgrave▶**pivot**

www.palgrave.com/pivot

1

A Pedagogy of Induction: Building Capacity

Abstract: *Henderson and Noble introduce a design-based research project conducted over seven years in a regional university in Australia. The research was designed as part of five scholarly teaching-learning projects. Some projects were established initially to address the attrition of early career teachers, by creating opportunities for professional induction and transition to the world of work. The projects inform thinking that initial teacher education programs should include a strong focus on professional learning and that such an approach will build workforce capacity over time. The chapter highlights the need for individuals to identify as members of the profession from the commencement of their Education studies, to ensure that their transition to the world of work is well supported and that the teacher workforce is sustainable.*

Keywords: design-based research; initial teacher education; professional induction; professional learning; transition; workforce capacity building

Henderson, Robyn and Karen Noble. *Professional Learning, Induction and Critical Reflection: Building Workforce Capacity in Education.* Basingstoke: Palgrave Macmillan, 2015. DOI: 10.10579781137473028.0004.

Introduction

The ideas for this book started about seven years ago, when our thinking about induction and professional learning in Education brought us to consider what we regarded as challenges for those working in initial teacher education. We were interested in how and when pre-service educators (students in the discipline of Education) began to think and act like 'teachers'. We were concerned when we heard statistics that suggested that the attrition of 'new' teachers was high and that many pre-service educators would not stay long term in the teaching workforce, despite their four years of Education study (Ewing & Manuel, 2005; Verstegen & Zhang, 2012).

Pre-service educators in Australia study Education at university, enrolling in a specified number of courses, which focus individually on what are regarded as critical learnings for future teachers. Most initial teacher education programs include courses about lifespan development and learning, curriculum and pedagogy, assessment and reporting, literacy and numeracy, and so on. Yet, we all know that the expected outcomes of initial teacher education are much more than this seemingly compartmentalised learning. When 'new' teachers move or transition into the profession, they are expected to be able to draw together all of their learnings and to work with 'whole' learners and 'whole' curricula. In teacher education programs, sometimes it is assumed that pre-service educators will know automatically how to integrate their vast knowledge from across courses, or that their professional experience, often called 'prac', will provide opportunities for them to do this. We see these assumptions as sometimes problematic.

At graduation, pre-service educators are expected to be ready to make the transition from university student, or pre-service educator, to professional teacher. However, if we are serious about wanting students to be, know and do (Gee, 1996) teaching, and to be able to integrate all that they know about teaching in a seamless way, then a transition or induction to the profession at the end of university study seems a little late. Our feeling – and, when we began to think about professional induction, it was no more than a feeling – was that induction into the teaching profession needed to start at the beginning of Education study, rather than being left until the end. Professional induction from the outset, where pre-service educators could learn how to think, be, do and know (Gee, 1996) like teachers, seemed to be an idea worthy

DOI: 10.1057/9781137473028.0004

of investigation. This seemed important in light of evidence that the attrition rate of teachers has been high, with as many as 40 per cent of beginning teachers leaving or intending to leave the profession within five years of becoming a teacher (Ewing & Manuel, 2005; Verstegen & Zhang, 2012).

Such alarming statistics were a stimulus for us to think further about what learning might be useful for pre-service educators in our University context. As teacher educators, we wanted to ensure that pre-service educators were prepared to tackle whatever challenges teaching was likely to present, particularly in today's climate of uncertainty, insecurity and unpredictability (Edwards, Ranson, & Strain, 2002). Initially, we wanted to enhance teaching and learning, but we also planned to incorporate research so that our work was research informed. We decided on a design-based research approach (Barab & Squire, 2004; The Design-Based Research Collective, 2003; Wang & Hannafin, 2005) which melded teaching and learning with research and allowed us to incorporate a strong focus on critical reflection (Macfarlane, Noble, Kilderry, & Nolan, 2006). We used the latter as a tool for students as well as for monitoring and assessing our own actions. In taking this approach, we set out to extend theoretical understandings beyond our local context (Barab & Squire, 2004).

This book, then, tells the story behind our professional induction project that has continued to morph as we have extended into new contexts. We see our approach, which provides a focus on process rather than content, as an important way to enhance professional learning and induction. Over time, our ideas have moved beyond the initial needs of our own context (Barab & Squire, 2004) – in relation to professional induction for pre-service educators – to consider the transfer of these ideas to professional learning more generally as an approach to building workforce capacity. Critical reflection has remained a mainstay. The result of our practice and research is what we have called a pedagogy of induction.

In this book, we describe the design-based research that has informed our work encompassing professional induction, professional learning and critical reflection. This first chapter outlines some insights into the context within which we operated. It then explains our chosen approach of design-based research, the multifaceted-research project that we conducted over seven years, and the five teaching-learning projects around which the research was shaped.

DOI: 10.1057/9781137473028.0004

The broad educational context

As teacher educators, our work is located in the higher education context of an Australian university. In education, today's world is dominated by mechanisms that measure and compare. It is clearly evident in Australia that neoliberal discourses have been operating in higher education and initial teacher education for some time. Our work as teacher educators has been impacted by the necessity for compliance with the requirements for teacher registration and teacher professional standards (Allard, Mayer, & Moss, 2014; Falabella, 2014). Yet despite these regulatory and accountability measures, recent political statements continue to pronounce teaching quality as a major social concern. In 2014, for example, an announcement by Australian Education Minister Christopher Pyne instigated a review of teacher education. According to Pyne (2014), teacher education is not 'attracting the top students into teacher courses' and 'courses are too theoretical, ideological and faddish'. Pyne's criticism of teacher quality and effectiveness and his push for teachers to be better prepared for classrooms frame teacher education in narrow and deficit terms. Indeed, from such a perspective, not only are graduating teachers regarded as deficient; so too are the teacher educators who teach them.

Pronouncements such as Pyne's, which focus narrowly on teacher effectiveness (Skourdoumbis, 2014), imply that there is a simple solution for what would seem to be a complex problem. Improving teacher effectiveness, for example, seems to be regarded as a panacea for all things wrong with teacher education and graduating teachers. Unfortunately, experience suggests that such simplistic solutions are often accompanied by reductionist approaches to curriculum and even teaching. What concerns us is that this context is the one that our pre-service educators will face as they move into the teaching workforce. We see it as important that they have deep understandings about their future 'work' as teachers/ educators and that they are able to articulate what they do and why. We base our thinking about professional induction on the assumption that future teachers will need to deal with the complexities of the teaching role as well as the complexities of the changing contexts of education.

It was in such times that our project originated and continues. Underpinning our project was our thinking that, through understanding the nexus between theory and practice and regarding themselves as members of the teaching profession from the beginning of their

DOI: 10.1057/9781137473028.0004

Education study, pre-service educators – future teachers – could collaboratively develop an ability to be, do and know teaching (Gee, 1996).

The research design

As already explained, our research project is an example of design-based research (Barab & Squire, 2004; The Design-Based Research Collective, 2003; Wang & Hannafin, 2005), drawing together our aims as practitioners (teachers of pre-service educators) and researchers. This form of research enabled us to incorporate both pragmatic and research aims (Wang & Hannafin, 2005) and to theorise practice and learning. It also assisted us to extend our work into various contexts with empirical evidence to support our actions. In doing this, we have been flexible in our use of methodologies and we have built theory as we have improved our own educational practice (The Design-Based Research Collective, 2003; Wang & Hannafin, 2005).

In using design-based research as our approach, we adopted the five principles described by Wang and Hannafin (2005). Firstly, our work was pragmatic, addressing practical issues that we regarded as important within the context of teacher education. We wanted to be sure that our students – pre-service educators – had opportunities to consider what have been called problems of practice (Ball & Cohen, 1999; Lampert, 1985) and to become cognisant of multiple ways that teachers might address such issues in their daily work. In other words, we wanted pre-service educators to engage with the types of issues that teachers face, whether they be problems that might occur in everyday practice (The Design-Based Research Collective, 2003), daily decision-making, pedagogical issues (Lampert, 1985), or contentious issues and topics that are taken up in the public arena as worthy of debate.

Secondly, our research was grounded in a real-life context. Our initial aim was to enhance opportunities for pre-service educators to synthesise aspects of their learning and to make clear links between theory and practice, but we also planned to investigate those opportunities and the outcomes for students by conducting research. Our project explored theoretical issues and practice, building on a research base about critical reflection (for example, Henderson, Noble, & Cross, 2013; Macfarlane et al., 2006; Ryan, 2012) and collaborative learning (for example, Gee, 1996; Lave & Wenger, 1999).

DOI: 10.1057/9781137473028.0004

Thirdly, our work incorporated an iterative design. As Wang and Hannafin (2005) identified, research-based design incorporates iterative cycles that encompass design, action, reflection and analysis, and redesign. Our practice was revised and refined as we reflected critically on what we were doing and the outcomes. With the integration of practice and research and the ongoing redesign, modification and refinement that were embedded in our approach, flexibility was necessarily a characteristic of our work. It was important to remember that design-based research takes place in real-life settings where predictability is never guaranteed (Barab & Squire, 2004). We always operated with a particular process in mind, but to others it may have seemed that our plans were in a form that Wang and Hannafin may have described as 'insufficiently detailed' (p. 7). However, this was essential to the way we wanted to work and the outcomes we wanted to achieve.

Fourthly, we drew on a range of methods to ensure that our research was responsive to the needs and issues that arose (Wang & Hannafin, 2005). We used a range of data collection tools, as will be explained in the next section, and a range of theoretical resources, in keeping our plan for our work to be informed by multiple perspectives. This will be evident through the chapters that follow.

Finally, context was an important component of our research approach. The projects we instigated were designed specifically for the teacher education context within which we were working, and changes to our approach were deliberately context-specific. However, as we began to work across different contexts within our University, we started to realise that the processes were probably transferable to professional learning contexts outside the University. As will be discussed in Chapter 6, our various projects indicated possibilities for transferability.

The research project

Over a seven-year period, we used a design-based research approach (Barab & Squire, 2004; The Design-Based Research Collective, 2003; Wang & Hannafin, 2005) to examine and theorise our practice. Although we discuss research in this section and our teaching-learning projects in the next section of this chapter, this separation is an artificial one. Our teaching-learning and research were inextricably connected, but we have separated them here for the sake of clarity and ease of reading.

DOI: 10.1057/9781137473028.0004

Our design-based research served three main purposes: to inform our current practice, to feed forward to our future practices and generate ideas for learning innovation, and to provide theories that could be shared with others (The Design-Based Research Collective, 2003) to enhance knowledge and theorisation beyond our local context. In order to accomplish these aims, we had multiple, participatory roles. We were teachers and facilitators of learning, designers and innovators, and researchers.

Most of our research was conducted in the University where we worked. Our work began initially in teacher education within a regional Australian university. However, as will become apparent in the section about our teaching-learning projects, we have extended into a global context, into another area of higher education, and into a schooling context where the focus was the professional learning of teachers. In all, five teaching-learning projects have informed our research.

We used multiple methods for collecting data during the projects. We privileged social interactions with participants as the major sources of qualitative data. These social practices (Mills, 2001), traditionally the techniques of ethnography, included informal conversations, focus-group discussions and semi-structured interviews with participants, as well as video- and audio-recorded discussions that occurred during some of the projects. These data were transcribed for analysis. We also used surveys and we kept extensive field and observation notes, which included our own reflections both in and on action (Schön, 1983).

The model of critical reflection (Macfarlane et al., 2006) that informed our teaching-learning practice also informed our research practice. The use of this model meant that we were analysing data continuously throughout the teaching–learning projects. This was important to the iterative process of data analysis that is part of both design-based research and critically reflective teaching practice. Our critical reflections incorporated the steps of theorising and thinking otherwise (Macfarlane et al., 2006), which worked to achieve the aims that were stated earlier: to inform our current practice, to feed forward to our future practices and generate ideas for learning innovation, and to build theory as a way of sharing our work beyond the local context and contributing theoretically to the field. To achieve our aims, we drew on a range of analytical tools. This will become evident throughout the remaining chapters.

DOI: 10.1057/9781137473028.0004

The teaching–learning projects

This section describes the teaching–learning projects that have been the focus of the research that informs this book. As has already been explained, over the past seven years we have been developing an approach to professional induction and a pedagogy of induction. In total, we have been involved in five projects which, although different in many aspects, have contributed to the thinking and research that we present here. All of the projects have been underpinned by a model of critical reflection (Macfarlane et al., 2006) and have augmented our understandings of professional learning and induction.

All five projects have contributed to our understandings about a pedagogy of induction, which developed as we conducted the projects. However, some projects more than others have provided us with evidence of how a pedagogy of induction can work 'in action'. For this reason, we describe the projects in this order:

▶ Project 1 (Education Commons) and Project 2 (Education Commons International) are examples of a pedagogy of induction in action, specifically as part of teacher education. We see the approach to professional induction as helping to develop workforce capacity.

▶ Project 3 (FYI Program) was the first project that we established in teacher education. It focused on the transition of students into the University context and it made significant contributions to our thinking about how a pedagogy of induction might work.

▶ Project 4 (Extending Education Commons into a school context) and Project 5 (Doc Chat) are examples of our use of the processes of a pedagogy of induction in other contexts. These projects have helped us to see how a pedagogy of induction might work in a range of contexts and contribute to the building of workforce capacity beyond teacher education.

Project 1: Education Commons

Of the five projects, the Education Commons project is one of the two projects that illustrate our approach to professional induction most clearly. Education Commons was established as a meeting place for pre-service educators, novice and experienced teachers, school administrators (for example, principals and deputy principals), and academics.

DOI: 10.1057/9781137473028.0004

Initially, Education Commons used a cyclical two-step process. The first step involved a panel of educators. Panel members came from a range of educational sectors that included early childhood, primary, middle and secondary schooling, as well as vocational and further education. Panel discussions were presented in face-to-face mode in front of an audience of on-campus pre-service educators and faculty academics. The conversations were video-recorded so that video artefacts could be made available to all of the pre-service educators enrolled in Education programs, regardless of their location or mode of study (Henderson et al., 2013).

Each panel event focused on a specific topic of educational interest. Where possible, we selected topics that were of interest to all participants, regardless of their teaching experience or the educational sector that they worked in or were expecting to work in. Sometimes the topics addressed educational change (for example, the introduction of new curriculum); sometimes they addressed controversial issues or focused on topics that were receiving extensive media attention (for example, the release of results for Australia's standardised testing; media discussions about a literacy crisis); at other times, they addressed topics of general interest to participants (for example, teaching in rural and remote contexts; behaviour management). In all cases, we expected that the focus topic would prompt diverse reactions from those who participated in the discussion and that multiple perspectives and multiple ways of thinking about and dealing with the issue would be embedded in the conversation. Each panel began with the panellists introducing themselves and explaining why the topic was relevant to them. From there, the conversation went wherever the panel or the audience took it. There was no set agenda and the audience was always invited to ask questions and to contribute to the discussion wherever possible.

The second step of the initial Education Commons process was a pedagogical conversation. Using the video-recordings from the panel discussion as stimulus materials, this conversation provided opportunities to revisit ideas from the panel discussion and to unpack some of those ideas (see Henderson et al., 2013). It also encouraged pre-service educators to reflect critically on that discussion, to link those ideas to their own experiences, and to think about how they might apply their learning to future experiences. The pedagogical conversations were available to all on-campus pre-service educators, regardless of whether they had attended the panel event or not.

DOI: 10.1057/9781137473028.0004

Both types of conversations – the panel discussions and the pedagogical conversations – were shaped around a model of critical reflection based on the work of Macfarlane et al. (2006). In facilitating the conversations, we ensured that the four stages of the model – deconstruct, confront, theorise and think otherwise – were considered. The model of critical reflection is discussed in depth in Chapter 2.

Although our initial implementation of Education Commons included panel discussions and pedagogical conversations, over time we conducted only the panel discussions. Even though we recognised that the pedagogical conversations drilled further into topics and enabled additional critical reflection and deep thinking about the topic that the panel had discussed, feedback from students suggested that they questioned the time commitment that was involved. Additionally, we were concerned that we could not make the pedagogical conversations available to all students and this presented us with an equity issue. In contrast to the panel discussions, which were video-recorded, made available to all students online and therefore could be accompanied by an online forum, the pedagogical conversations did not lend themselves to an asynchronous online environment. At that time, the technology available to us did not allow us to find a way of addressing that problem, so we continued with the panel discussions only.

Project 2: Education Commons International

Collaboration with a colleague from an overseas University and her visit to our University fostered some initial discussions about how to extend Education Commons from our local context into a global context. After investigating the technological possibilities of linking the two universities, we decided to trial an Education Commons International. Our first attempt was successful and this resulted in the linking of the two universities two times per year for a panel event. Using video-conferencing to link the two locations, we operated with half the panel – usually three panel members – in our University and the other half in the University in the USA, with an audience in both locations. The synchronous conversation moved backwards and forwards between locations, with panel members and the audiences engaging in discussions on the focus topic.

Although the same process was followed as has already been described for Education Commons (Project 1), the difference, of course, was that the discussion addressed the nominated topic from the perspectives of pre-service educators and professional teachers in two very different

DOI: 10.1057/9781137473028.0004

contexts – a regional location in Australia and an urban location in the USA. Although there were substantial differences in the university and school contexts, many of the participants in these discussions commented on the similarities relating to education and the challenges facing teachers in current times.

Project 3: the FYI Program

The fourth project was one that we originally called the First Year Infusion Program – FYI for short. This was a support program for self-identified, at-risk, on-campus students who were enrolled in the first year of an Education degree. Initially, the program was established in response to concerns about the retention and progression of university students across the sector. However, we made changes to the program and offered the second iteration to all first year Education students. Later, in response to requests from students, we offered the program to all on-campus students who were studying Education, regardless of their stage of study. At that point, we changed the name of the program, with the new name, For Your Information, maintaining FYI as the acronym.

In all iterations of the program, we offered a weekly, two-hour meeting that operated as a learning circle (Lovett & Gilmore, 2003; Noble & Henderson, 2008; Noble, Macfarlane, & Cartmel, 2006; Ravensbergen & VanderPlaat, 2010). As we have described in other publications (for example, Henderson & Noble, 2009; Henderson, Noble, & De George-Walker, 2009; Noble & Henderson, 2008), this pedagogical approach engaged students in critical reflection on what they were experiencing and on their ways of doing, being and knowing at university (Henderson & Noble, 2009). By involving students in a learning community that included sharing and comparing, as well as negotiating and problem-solving (Henderson et al., 2009), the approach built on Tinto's (2008) encouragement for approaches that involve collaboration and collaborative learning.

The learning circle meeting created a safe environment in which students were able to discuss their experiences of university and the challenges or issues that were concerning them at the time. As explained in a paper that we wrote with De George-Walker (Henderson et al., 2009), many of the students were mature age, had experienced some type of interruption in their study, or were having a second attempt at university study. Additionally, they were attempting to manage their complex home lives as well as their study. The program emphasised social support and the learning community as ways to ensure academic success, thereby promoting social integration and just-in-time academic support. Through this approach, students' strengths were foregrounded, thus helping to shift deficit discourses about the students. The problem-solving approach of the learning circle helped students to use their strengths and capabilities from their lives outside the University to address some of the challenges they were experiencing in the University context.

Although initially we were the only University staff involved in the learning circle, as time went on we encouraged others to join us. Other academics, learning support staff and our faculty librarian attended on a regular basis. On some occasions, we invited staff to join us for a specific purpose. Sometimes some of the students invited particular academic staff to attend, as they had specific questions that they wanted to ask of them.

Within the learning circle, the students were encouraged to regard themselves as prospective teachers from the outset. The focus of the program, however, was on the student role and being a successful university student, as an important step in becoming a teacher. There was no set agenda for any of the meetings, as we wanted to work with whatever issues or challenges the students thought were important at the time. The program was underpinned by a model of critical reflection (Macfarlane et al., 2006) and we used this model to facilitate conversations within the learning circle. Our learnings from using the model of critical reflection and from employing an unstructured agenda were important to our thinking about Education Commons (Project 1), which was established after the FYI Program had been operating for two years.

Initially, we did not think about professional induction being a major part of the FYI Program. However, as we worked across the teaching–learning projects, we came to realise that the FYI Program was the beginning of our thinking about professional induction. We began to understand that pre-service educators make multiple transitions from the beginning of their university study until they move into the teaching profession. All of these contribute to their personal and professional identities.

Project 4: Extending Education Commons into a school context

One of our more recent projects has been the application of the Education Commons way of working into a context outside a university and involving a cluster of approximately 15 schools. The teachers and principals of these schools were interested in professional learning on the topic of school literacies. At present, there is considerable pressure on Australian schools to perform well on national literacy tests, which form part of the National Assessment Program – Literacy and Numeracy (NAPLAN). In this context of high stakes testing (Klenowski & Wyatt-Smith, 2012), the schools were implementing strategies and approaches, aiming to enhance their schools' literacy scores. However, the professional development that was on offer for teachers and principals located in the regional centre, where some of the schools were located, was difficult to access by those in rural and remote locations. As a result, the schools were looking for an innovative way for connecting and sharing practice, without having to fund the enormous travel costs that are often involved for schools in remote locations.

As part of this project, three panel discussions were conducted, using the format that we had used in Education Commons and Education Commons International. It was recognised that not all teachers and principals would be able to attend in person. However, to ensure accessibility for personnel of all 15 schools, the panel discussions were video-streamed in real time, with an opportunity to email questions for the panel to answer, and they were also made available on a website for viewing at a later date. These options provided flexibility for school personnel, particularly those in rural and remote locations.

It also meant that the video-recordings could be used by school personnel as stimulus materials or 'sparks' for professional learning in their own contexts. During the course of the project, video and photographic illustrations of literacy teaching and learning were added to the online repository of video-recordings. This enabled and enhanced the sharing of ideas across schools.

The panel discussions facilitated critical reflection on literacy learning, as well as the sharing of approaches and strategies. To provide further opportunities for school personnel to engage in professional learning, the project also included a series of webinars. These discussions could be accessed from any location by teachers and principals in participating schools, as long as they had a connection to the internet. The webinars offered opportunities to share ideas across contexts and to reflect critically on practice. As with our other projects, we used the model of critical reflection (Macfarlane et al., 2006) to frame discussions, to stimulate deep understandings that questioned and critiqued practice and theory, and to provide multiple perspectives on the topic at hand.

DOI: 10.1057/9781137473028.0004

Project 5: Doc Chat

The fifth project involved a regular meeting of doctoral students who were undertaking research in the field of education. We did not establish these meetings, but one of us took on a faculty role as a doctoral programs coordinator, thus inheriting an already established regularly occurring event. Although the initial purpose of the meeting was to allow the coordinator to touch base with on-campus doctoral students on a regular basis, the event developed into a self-sustaining learning community that seemed to meet the academic and social needs of the students who attended.

The fortnightly meetings have continued and have been framed by critical reflection. As with the FYI Program, there is no set agenda and attendance is voluntary. The students talk about their study, their achievements and their challenges. They share ideas, readings and references to the literature, and they sometimes ask others for suggestions or advice when they are experiencing particular research problems. Although we do not deal in depth with this project as part of this book, we regard it as an example of the implementation of a pedagogy of induction in a context outside teacher education.

The structure of the book

In this chapter, we have described the teaching–learning projects that we conducted over seven years and how we used design-based research to inform our work. In Chapter 2, we discuss the theoretical underpinnings of our projects. In particular, we describe the foundational tenets of learning and professional learning that inform our work in the five projects, as well as the model of critical reflection which is adapted from the work of McFarlane et al. (2006). In Chapters 3, 4 and 5, we use the stages of the model of critical reflection to unpack a pedagogy of induction. Chapter 3 discusses 'deconstruct' and 'confront'. Chapter 4 focuses on 'theorise' and Chapter 5 explores 'thinking otherwise'. In each of these chapters, we discuss and analyse some research data that were collected as part of the projects. We also talk about our learnings and the implications of our findings. In Chapter 6, the final chapter, we review our learnings about a pedagogy of induction and consider the implications for building workforce capacity.

DOI: 10.1057/9781137473028.0004

Because of the inherent complexities of conducting multiple projects linking teaching-learning and research, it is important that we explain upfront that the descriptions we provide in this book are 'unmessy' versions of what we did. Because many of our teaching-learning projects were running concurrently and the research was iterative, we have avoided a chronological telling. Whilst we are cognisant that design-based research is often characterised by complexity and messiness (Barab & Squire, 2004, p. 4), we have tried to provide some clarity for readers by being as unmessy as possible.

DOI: 10.1057/9781137473028.0004

2
Foundations of a Pedagogy of Induction

Abstract: *This chapter describes the foundational tenets of a pedagogy of induction, which was developed through a design-based research approach that investigated and advanced the effectiveness of five teaching–learning projects. A model of critical reflection, which was used to inform the teaching–learning projects as well as the research, enables an unpacking of the pedagogy through a researcher conversation. In doing this, the chapter provides insights into how the teaching–learning projects were established and highlights the multiple ways in which collaborative critical reflection can facilitate a rethinking of practice, a reimagining of future practice and a thinking forward to new projects and new theories.*

Keywords: critical reflection; Discourse; funds of knowledge; pedagogy of induction; social interactions; transformative learning

Henderson, Robyn and Karen Noble. *Professional Learning, Induction and Critical Reflection: Building Workforce Capacity in Education.* Basingstoke: Palgrave Macmillan, 2015. DOI: 10.1057/9781137473028.0005.

DOI: 10.1057/9781137473028.0005

Introduction

This chapter begins by describing the theoretical framing of our teaching–learning projects and the research accompanying them. In particular, it discusses the tenets about learning that inform a pedagogy of induction. It also describes and explains the model of critical reflection that has been adapted, from the work of Macfarlane, Noble, Kilderry, and Nolan (2006) through its use (Henderson, 2012; Henderson et al., 2013; Noble & McIlveen, 2012), as the practice framework for a pedagogy of induction and as a research tool.

After discussing the tenets underpinning the projects we described in Chapter 1, we present a conversation between ourselves as researchers. The conversation is typical of data produced as part of our long-term, design-based research approach, where critical reflection was used as a research tool. By providing a framework for deconstructing, confronting, theorising and thinking otherwise (Macfarlane et al., 2006), the model of critical reflection enabled modifications to the practice of our teaching–learning projects, as well as providing a tool for research purposes. We analyse the conversation in terms of the theories that we present, demonstrating insights into the collaborative culture that developed as part of the projects that we instigated.

Making sense of learning in a pedagogy of induction

In thinking about a pedagogy of induction we based our ideas on a number of understandings about learning. In particular, we recognised that:

▸ all learners have strengths which can be used as foundations for learning;
▸ induction into a profession involves learning a new Discourse (Gee, 1996) and taking on a new identity;
▸ social interactions provide opportunities for learning;
▸ critical reflection opens up the potential for problem-solving in new situations; and
▸ learning is transformative and allows the transfer of understandings from one context to another (Kalantzis, Cope, & the Learning by Design Project Group, 2005).

DOI: 10.1057/9781137473028.0005

We will now discuss each of these tenets about learning that provide the foundations to a pedagogy of induction and the theory that supports those ideas.

Learners' strengths

One of the basic tenets of our approach to a pedagogy of induction is that students, including pre-service educators, do not arrive at university *tabula rasa*. Rather, they come with a wealth of knowledge from their lives and their experiences outside the university. As Gonzales, Moll and Amanti (2005) highlighted, 'people are competent, they have knowledge, and their life experiences have given them that knowledge' (pp. ix–x). In other words, all students bring 'funds of knowledge' (Gonzales, Moll, & Amanti, 2005b; Moll, Amanti, Neff, & Gonzales, 1992) to their learning. Research has shown, however, that students' funds of knowledge are not always visible to those who teach them, because some knowledge seems to carry little value in formal educational settings and tends to be left outside or to remain hidden from those with teaching responsibilities (Henderson, 2004; Kocatepe, 2004; Thomson, 2002).

Although Gonzales, Moll and Amanti's (Gonzales et al., 2005b; Moll et al., 1992) explanations of funds of knowledge relate to school students and their lives outside of schools, the concept seems applicable to the university context. Indeed, university entry requirements generally invoke procedures that select students with particular backgrounds valorised by universities. Such procedures privilege particular types of prior knowledge and learning, and in turn – albeit unintentionally – can render other forms of knowledge as unimportant and invisible.

We recognise, of course, that university students bring a range of funds of knowledge to the university context. These include their lived experiences of home and community, of school education, and of university education. In the case of pre-service educators studying in teacher education faculties or involved in professional experience in schools, there is an expectation that they will build forms of knowledge relevant to their future careers as teachers. These knowledges have been clustered and described in various ways – as theory and practice, as content knowledge and pedagogical knowledge, and so on.

In our conceptualisation of a pedagogy of induction, we want pre-service educators to draw on their funds of knowledge. By using what they already know as the foundations for learning how to be a

DOI: 10.1057/9781137473028.0005

teacher, they are able to make links between 'the known' and 'the new' (Kalantzis et al., 2005). Such an approach, used within the model of critical reflection that is described later in this chapter (Henderson, 2012; Henderson et al., 2013; Macfarlane et al., 2006), allows for knowledge to be questioned and challenged, for theorising practice, and for seeing that multiple perspectives are both possible and useful.

Learning a new Discourse

A key tenet of a pedagogy of induction is that induction into a profession involves learning a new Discourse (Gee, 1996). Gee (1996) identifies a Discourse, with a capital D, as 'a usually taken for granted and tacit "theory" of what count as a "normal" person and the "right" ways to think, feel, and behave' (p. ix). Thus, Gee's conceptualisation gives us insights into the features of particular social groups, such as teachers, and their particular ways of 'being in the world', including believing, speaking, thinking, interacting, valuing and so on (p. viii).

In creating a pedagogy of induction, we wanted our program to work to develop the capabilities of pre-service educators to 'be' teachers, to understand themselves as belonging to the education profession, and to become educators who are able to cope with the dynamic nature of today's educational world. We saw the pedagogy as a process of induction, as a way of enabling pre-service educators to join a particular Discourse community. However, we also recognised that there might be benefits for others who became involved in one of the communities that we established, such as academic staff members and novice and experienced educators or teachers. These benefits included the affordances of shared knowledge and experience and the possibility of taking on new understandings and plans for future action – for continuing to 'be' effective teachers.

Teacher professional identity is a concept with a multitude of definitions (Beijaard, Meijer, & Verloop, 2004; Davey, 2013) and can be understood as individualistic and collective. Pre-service educators need space and opportunity to develop personal and professional identities as they engage in the complex process of integrating their 'new' professional self with their personal self (Alsup, 2006). The learning journey towards 'becoming' a teacher for contemporary education contexts is complex and dynamic in nature and as such has led to a plethora of research into teacher professional identity (for example, Beauchamp & Thomas, 2009; Calderhead & Shorrock, 1997; Chong, Low, & Goh, 2011; Clandinin &

DOI: 10.1057/9781137473028.0005

Connelly, 1996; Flores & Day, 2006; Sachs, 2005; Temmerman, Noble, & Danaher, 2010; Thomas & Beauchamp, 2007).

Taking the perspective that induction to the profession needs to commence at the beginning of teacher preparation programs, rather than upon entry into the actual workforce, this book is an attempt to explore the ways in which a collective approach to professional learning works to build capacity at all levels – individually as well as across the broader education workforce. We also argue that the journey of 'becoming' and 'being' a teacher is lifelong and involves ongoing growth and change, and therefore it should be the focus of professional learning across all career stages.

Social interactions enhance learning

In discussing the learning of a new Discourse and how to 'be' an educator or teacher, we have been addressing the issue of identity (Gee, 1996). However, as Gee (2014) highlighted, language serves multiple purposes. It not only 'allows us to be things ... to take on different socially significant identities' (p. 235), but it also allows us 'to inform each other' and 'to do things ... to engage in actions and activities' (p. 235). We regard these aspects of language and social interactions as foundational to our conceptualisation of a pedagogy of induction. Social interactions provide opportunities to make connections between saying, doing and being – that is, between informing, action and identity (Gee, 2014).

By setting up situations to facilitate social interactions, we were also helping to establish learning communities that could consider shared issues (Choi, 2013; Hollins, 2011; Tam, 2015). Gee (1996) emphasised the importance of incorporating opportunities to acquire Discourse through using it, as well as opportunities to develop a meta-knowledge through questioning, critiquing, explaining and analysing. As will become evident later in this chapter, we used a model of critical reflection to frame social interactions between the members of the learning communities of our projects – pre-service, novice and experienced educators, as well as academics. These social interactions – discussions – occurred in a supportive and non-judgemental place, where participants could feel safe and able to share their thinking about their experiences (Gonzales, Moll, & Amanti, 2005a).

Gee's (2004) considerations of learning suggest that 'specialist languages and their concomitant ways of thinking' – including the

DOI: 10.1057/9781137473028.0005

Discourse of being a teacher – are learnt best when learners 'can tie the words and structures of those languages to experiences they have had' (p. 4). In working on a pedagogy of induction, we deliberately created spaces for discussions amongst different educational stakeholders, including pre-service educators, experienced and novice teachers, principals and academics. In doing this, we were creating an affinity space (Gee, 2004; Henderson & Hirst, 2007) for conversations about particular experiences, such as those related to teaching or to being an Education student in a university. As Gee argued, affinity spaces enable interactions amongst those with 'common interests, endeavours, goals, or practices' as well as between 'newbies and masters' (p. 85).

Gee (2004) explained that this bringing together of a 'continuum of people from new to experienced, from unskilled to highly skilled' enables learning, and participants are able to 'get different things out of the space – based on their own choices, purposes, and identities' (p. 85). In some learning spaces, novices and experts are segregated, but the mingling that affinity spaces afford is effective for encouraging the sharing of intensive (specialised) knowledge and extensive (less specialised, broader) knowledge (Gee, 2004, p. 86). As Gee emphasised, affinity spaces enable the sharing of knowledge of different types. Indeed, some knowledge may be tacit – knowledge which participants have 'built up in practice, but may not be able to explicate fully in words' (p. 86).

Incorporating critical reflection

In designing a pedagogy of induction, we were able to use the concept of an affinity space (Gee, 2004) to open spaces for discussion, to encourage sharing, and to facilitate learning. We regarded critical reflection as a significant aspect of this learning. As Mortari (2012) noted, reflection has been regarded as an important activity in professional life and is often regarded as 'a necessary condition for acquiring expertise' (p. 525). Smith and Trede (2013) suggested that reflective practice is often seen as an 'entry-level practice for the professions' (p. 632). Indeed, in the teaching field, there has been a long tradition of support for reflection and this is evident in extensive literature (for example, Boud & Walker, 1998; Dewey, 1933; Schön, 1983; Zeichner & Liston, 1996).

Reflection is sometimes described as an individual practice that is useful for making the transition to 'competent professional' who is able to use knowledge from experience. However, it is widely recognised

DOI: 10.1057/9781137473028.0005

that reflection is also 'contextual, particular and social' (Smith & Trede, 2013, p. 638). Indeed, according to Smith and Trede (2013), reflection may be more social than individualistic. However, for pre-service educators whose time is divided between different contexts – the university, community and schools, for example – opportunities to bring different contexts together seem important.

Zeichner (2010) highlighted disconnections between university- and school-based aspects of teacher education programs as one of the 'problems that have plagued college- and university-based pre-service teacher education' (p. 89) for a long time. In fact, we regularly hear claims that teacher education is too theoretical. As has been noted elsewhere (for example, Kuusisaari, 2013; Sjølie, 2014; Zeichner, 2010), pre-service educators are often faced with the dilemma of making sense of their practical experiences in schools in relation to the theoretical work they do in the university context. Zeichner (2010) suggested that a way of overcoming this disconnect it to create hybrid spaces where 'academic and practitioner knowledge and knowledge that exists in communities come together in new less hierarchical ways in the service of teacher learning' (p. 89). This means shifting the epistemology of teacher education from being '*the* authoritative source of knowledge about teaching' to one where 'different aspects of expertise that exist in schools and communities are brought into teacher education and coexist on a more equal plane with academic knowledge' (p. 95).

We regard critical reflection as a tool that can enable learning at the nexus of theory and practice and will allow considerations of theory to inform practice and considerations of practice to inform understandings about theory. By offering a space – in line with the types of places suggested by Zeichner (2010) and Gee (2004) – critical reflection can result in the bringing together of theoretical and practitioner knowledges, as well as a range of explicit and tacit knowledges.

We are aware that there has been some problematising of reflection and critical reflection and that a diversity of reflective approaches exists (Hickson, 2011). However, we are also cognisant of the insecurity, uncertainty and unpredictability surrounding contemporary working environments (Edwards et al., 2002) and the importance of pre-service educators having the capabilities to work within such contexts. It seemed to us that pre-service educators need to develop capabilities to think through problems that relate to their practice, to be able to draw on a range of resources including theoretical resources, and to see that there

DOI: 10.1057/9781137473028.0005

are often multiple solutions to the problems and issues that they may face as educators.

This links with Kalantzis and Cope's (n.d.) understandings about the development of repertoires of practice. They define these as 'the sum of available tools, techniques, strategies, tactics, ways of working, expertise and know-how from which a practitioner may draw, choose from, and/ or combine to suit both known and novel situations or address a particular purpose'. Participants in learning communities can bring and share diverse views, skills and practices. However, critical reflection enables the interrogation of ideas, skills and practices that might be taken-for-granted or normalised in particular contexts, thus opening the way for 'multiple understandings, theoretically and practically' (Macfarlane et al., 2006, p. 14).

'Problems of practice' seem to provide useful starting points for pre-service educators who, after all, are working towards becoming education professionals and practitioners. Issues that are 'intimately embedded in practice' (O'Connell Rust, 2009, p. 1883) are useful for reflecting on and rethinking the theory-practice nexus. If the building of these capacities is important, then we need to find a process for developing these complex capabilities, thereby ensuring that pre-service educators have ways of conceptualising and evaluating possible courses of action.

We argue, therefore, for critical reflection that incorporates both theory and practice, as well as tacit and explicit knowledge, thus moving beyond an uncritical observation of self towards a process that helps to mobilise thoughts, theories, ideas and discourses through interactions (Noble & McIlveen, 2012). We see this approach as necessarily collaborative and as a way of enabling pre-service educators to understand, create, affirm and sustain ways of being, knowing and doing 'teacher' and 'teaching' (Gee, 1996; Noble & McIlveen, 2012). In using such a process, we highlight the potential to empower pre-service educators and novice and experienced teachers and to position them as agentic subjects who can resist discourses of power and control (Noble & McIlveen, 2012). It was such a plan that informed the original development of the model of critical reflection (Macfarlane et al., 2006) and the further refinement of the model across a range of contexts (for example, Henderson & Noble, 2013; Henderson et al., 2013; Noble & Henderson, 2008, 2012), where the focus has been specifically on how problems of identity and difference are constructed within social and political contexts.

DOI: 10.1057/9781137473028.0005

A model of critical reflection

We drew on a particular model of critical reflection from the work of Macfarlane, Noble, Kilderry, and Nolan (2006). The model incorporates four stages and provides opportunities to think deeply about problems of practice, to make links between theory and practice, and to think about other possibilities for educational practice (Henderson et al., 2013). The four stages of the model – deconstruct, confront, theorise and think otherwise – offer a useful framework for making sure that the reflection goes beyond the superficial to be deep, active and critical. As Ryan (2012) argued, this ensures that critical reflection works on two levels. At one level, participants can make sense of their experiences. At the other level, they are 'reimagining future experience' (Ryan, 2012, p. 208).

The inclusion of a critical element is important for incorporating what might be called 'self-doubt' (Nicholas, 2015) or 'a position of doubt' that will make the focus 'object or idea appear problematic, tentative, plural, multiple and complex' (Patterson, 1997, p. 425). As Ryan (2012) highlighted, more abstract, higher level and critical reflection, which she calls academic or professional reflection, facilitates those engaged in the reflection to make sense of experience. She identifies this as happening in several ways:

- understanding the context of learning and the particular issues;
- understanding one's own contribution to that context, including past experiences, values/philosophies and knowledge;
- drawing on other evidence or explanation from the literature or relevant theories;
- using all of this knowledge to re-imagine and ultimately improve future experience (from Ryan, 2012, p. 209).

As a way of establishing conversational routines across the various learning communities that form our design-based research approach, the stages of the model of critical reflection – deconstruct, confront, theorise and think otherwise (Noble et al., 2006) – are made explicit to project participants from the outset. Each stage of the model has a particular intention. These are:

1 to *deconstruct* teaching issues and practices, including problems of practice. This requires a pulling apart or analysis of what has or might happen in practice, especially practices that are taken-for-granted and have become normalised, and the dominant discourses that are circulating;

DOI: 10.1057/9781137473028.0005

2   to *confront* particular aspects of those issues and practices, thus examining difficult and sometimes 'untouchable' topics. This stage asks questions about what aspects of practice might need to be changed;

3   to *theorise* by drawing on theory and linking it to practice. This stage requires broad thinking, going beyond practice to identify theories, other discourses, relevant research and evidence;

4   to *think otherwise* by challenging oneself to think beyond dominant discursive frameworks, thus identifying other ways of thinking about and practising 'teacher' and 'teaching'. This stage accepts multiple perspectives and options for practice (adapted from Macfarlane et al., 2006, p. 16).

These four stages promote a culture of critical evaluation, thus engaging learning community members in a review of what is happening and what could be happening. The first two stages serve to trouble practice and to apply a condition of doubt (Patterson, 1997), thereby 'unravelling the meanings and discourses embedded in our sense-making and narratives' (Bay & Macfarlane, 2011, p. 748). The other two stages help to reconstruct practice by drawing 'on other evidence or explanation from the literature or relevant theories' (Ryan, 2012, p. 209) and thinking about multiple practice possibilities. By working through all four stages, participants move beyond acceptance and maintenance of the status quo (Gur-Ze'ev, Masschelein, & Blake, 2001) towards rethinking and reimagining how practice might be. These stages have obvious synergies with Ryan's (2012) list of the range of ways that academic or professional reflection can happen.

The model is not only used by members of the community, but it also frames the way in which the learning communities are facilitated. Given the changing membership of the learning communities, it is essential that the model can be simply and quickly articulated so that it can be adopted easily by all in structuring the event. If taught and practised effectively, critical reflection can act as a means of deconstructing traditional ways of being, knowing and doing teacher and teaching. It can also help to explore and consider ways of being, knowing and doing that may delimit possibilities for future-focused, well-informed and socially responsive practice, and to reconsider such approaches and what might be 'done' differently. Therefore, inherent in our ways of working across this design-based research is the view that the model of critical reflection provides the structure for the conversational routines across each of the programs as well as being the framework that is practised explicitly

DOI: 10.1057/9781137473028.0005

by all participants. As such, the 'walk' and the 'talk' are achieved through the structure of the model of critical reflection.

Transformative learning

A pedagogy of induction is a transformative process. It promotes active learning, whereby participants engage in discussions that enhance understandings about how to improve learning and about how to improve professional practice (Ryan, 2012). Kalantzis, Cope and the Learning by Design Project Group (2005) highlighted two important conditions of learning. In simple terms, they argued that learning will not occur unless learners feel a sense of belonging – that is, that 'the learning is for them' (p. 43) – and that learning takes learners away from their comfort zone (p. 47) and enables both personal and cultural transformation (p. 48). Indeed, an important aspect of a pedagogy of induction is that learning can be applied to both familiar and unfamiliar contexts. This links to the strengths-based approach that we outlined when talking about learner strengths, as well as the need for learning to result in some form of transformation. As Kalantzis et al. explained, the application of learning can occur 'in unexceptional ways in the everyday realm of the lifeworld,' whether that is by applying knowledge appropriately or applying it creatively (p. 78). In a pedagogy of induction, the aim is for participants to consider their experiences in current contexts and to re-imagine future experiences (Ryan, 2012). In doing this, they are also able to consider how they might operate in new contexts and with new experiences.

Critical reflection as a research tool

To conclude this chapter, we share part of our ongoing conversations as researchers using a design-based research approach. During the years that we conducted the projects that contribute to this book, we used critical reflection as a research tool to reflect on our practice and on the way that the projects were unfolding. We deconstructed, confronted, theorised and thought otherwise (Macfarlane et al., 2006). These four stages of the model of critical reflection enabled us to fine-tune, to rethink our practice, to re-imagine the projects' futures, and to think forward to what might become new projects at a future time.

In this section of the chapter, then, we present the transcript of a conversation where we reflect critically on our experiences of conducting the projects over several years. We also reflect on the tenets underpinning

DOI: 10.1057/9781137473028.0005

a pedagogy of induction. For ease of understanding, however, we have used a '*said it and edit* process' (Henderson & Lennon, 2014, p. 120) to edit the conversation for an audience wider than ourselves. The transcripts are representative of our critical reflections during the projects, although in this case the reflections are across several projects rather than in relation to a single project.

The editing of the transcript allowed us to enhance readability by eliminating pauses, confusing statements and irrelevant information, as well as to reorder sections and to add details, thus ensuring that readers are able to understand the context and our thinking. In adding details, we have incorporated data from other sources, including recorded conversations and remembered conversations, as well as our notes taken during the projects, published writing and award nominations. In effect, the transcript presented here combines academic research with autobiographic ethnography (Lather & Smithies, 1997), framed within the model of critical reflection.

Data analysis is embedded in the process of critical reflection. However, for ease of presentation and readability, we have also provided an accompanying analytical and explanatory commentary to some sections of the transcript. The commentary functions like a 'voiceover' (see Henderson & Lennon, 2014), to draw overall conclusions from the transcript data about a set of particular research questions. The questions we address are:

▸ How does the process of critical reflection support a pedagogy of induction?
▸ How did the projects draw on learners' strengths?
▸ What did we learn about Gee's (1996) concept of Discourse and 'becoming' a teacher?
▸ How did social interactions provide opportunities for learning?
▸ Did the projects achieve their aims for transformative learning?
▸ What are the implications for teacher education and the world of work?

Reflecting on our research journey

Our conversation has three sections which identify three particular stages in our journey through the five teaching–learning projects and the associated design-based research:

▸ The beginning: The FYI Program (Project 3)

DOI: 10.1057/9781137473028.0005

▸ Building a pedagogy of induction: Education Commons (Project 1)
▸ Extending into new contexts: Projects 2, 4 and 5.

The beginning: the FYI Program (Project 3)

We start our conversation by talking about the FYI Program. This was in fact our first project and it played a major role in developing the ideas that underpin a pedagogy of induction.

Robyn: I keep thinking about how we have used critical reflection as part of our practice in organising all of these projects, but also as a tool for research. That's important.

Karen: Yes it is.

Robyn: Over all these years we've reflected on our practice – how we've conducted particular events within our projects and on how things worked or didn't work. That reflection has become part of what we do, how we work, who we are.

Karen: That's probably not surprising, though. We've both been using the model of critical reflection in our teaching for years.

Robyn: That's true.

Karen: We do critical reflection in all of our work – personal and professional.

Robyn: It's interesting to think back to how we started. Remember how we began the FYI Program? Our first collaboration. And a rushed job! A quick corridor conversation, a few rushed plans and the FYI Program was up and running!

Karen: And then we changed those plans!

Robyn: That would seem to be a perfect example of critical reflection in action and the effect of design-based research. We learnt so much in those early days. We tried an approach, then learnt what aspects worked and which ones didn't.

Karen: And what the students thought. Their feedback highlighted the importance of listening to students and their needs for learning. We also had to adjust to the new practice context we were in, with both of us being quite new to the institution and learning the rules of engagement as academics in this context. Mostly though our focus was on understanding our students and their learning needs.

DOI: 10.1057/9781137473028.0005

Robyn: And the need to learn what strengths they brought with them, their funds of knowledge.

Karen: We deconstructed and confronted issues around what would work for students who were 'at risk' of being unsuccessful in the university context.

Robyn: We learnt a lot from the students, didn't we?

Karen: Yes. Our plans for a program that provided academic support were thrown out immediately.

Robyn: At the time, I was surprised by the way that the students saw social issues as their main issue.

Karen: In hindsight, though, that has taught us a lot. The importance of relationships and relational pedagogy.

Robyn: And those ideas resulted in thinking about how we might make links to the literature, to theorise – another stage of the model of critical reflection.

Karen: And the importance of thinking otherwise, of understanding that not all support programs have to work in the same way.

As we explained in Chapter 1, the FYI Program was constructed around a learning circle approach (Lovett & Gilmore, 2003; Noble & Henderson, 2008; Ravensbergen & VanderPlaat, 2010). Our intent in establishing the program was to provide a safe environment for problem-solving, to demonstrate to the pre-service educators that their strengths would enable them to find solutions to the difficulties they were experiencing, and to encourage critical reflection as a useful framework to guide their thinking (Henderson & Noble, 2009; Henderson et al., 2009; Noble & Henderson, 2008). We used the model of critical reflection (Macfarlane et al., 2006) to frame our discussions with students as well as to frame our reflections on our practice.

Karen: From the very beginning it was clear that the challenges to face were mammoth – for the students and for us. When we began FYI we quickly realised that it needed to be about fit for purpose. We also learned a lot about being flexible and adaptable – to be responsive to students rather than being as proactive as we would normally have been in supporting students' induction into the university context.

DOI: 10.1057/9781137473028.0005

Robyn: Strange, isn't it? As teachers, we tend to think that being proactive is best. We usually consider what we think students' learning needs are, then design our teaching to cater for those needs.

Karen: Yet FYI taught us that we couldn't really pre-plan, because we needed to respond to the needs that the students identified.

Robyn: So true. While we were able to scaffold certain key academic skills into the sessions, it was clear that we were most successful when we allowed the questions, ideas and issues to emerge from the students and then to work forward from there.

Karen: We also worked hard to build the social cohesion of the group process. Although the membership changed from week to week – after all, student attendance was voluntary – the consistency and I think the comfort for the students emerged through our adherence to the structure of the model of critical reflection and also in reinforcing the learning circle approach in terms of its democratic underpinnings.

Robyn: From the feedback and ongoing engagement we have had with the students, it is apparent that the lack of judgement or assessment was a comfort to them. They did not feel the need to perform in a particular way.

Karen: Yes, actually that proved critical I think. The students saw the space as a safe haven and I remember how they used metaphors like 'a lifebuoy', 'a space to escape from university' and the like.

Robyn: They also over time saw us as guides on the side. We developed a collegial relationship with them very quickly really. They learned to trust us and, in fact, remember the time when they arrived and as a group confronted us about what they could do for us rather than it always being about what we did for them?

Karen: That was a major event when you think back. That was where the research aspect came from actually. That was when the importance of the social – the privileging of interactions and relationships – became apparent. For my thinking it was also where we were able to illustrate to the students the importance of mutually beneficial collaborations. Their engagement in research, as first-year students, was quite profound, especially when you think that they had self-identified as 'at-risk' students in joining with us.

DOI: 10.1057/9781137473028.0005

Robyn: That first group within FYI were amazing – the way that they connected and the fact that, as time went on, they actually practised the model of critical reflection themselves in the study group that they formed. That group met regularly between the FYI sessions.

Karen: Yes. They used the model themselves to solve all kinds of problems – social and academic in fact. Like the time that one of them found herself homeless. Remember how they came to us after they had already convened to try to collectively come up with possible solutions?

Robyn: They were able to prioritise and collectively act to support one another in many different situations.

Karen: Like the times when Catherine (pseudonym) would talk about her car as the only space to escape on the university campus. And how many times she thought of turning the key and fleeing from university back to her safe space at home.

Robyn: That's right. And how, once she shared that story, some of the others helped to brainstorm alternative strategies to support her survival, her transition into university. That was how their daily library study group began!

Karen: From there that group went from strength to strength. Once they realised that others were there to help and support them – but also that others needed them to do likewise – they had a purpose, they set goals and they became accountable to each other

Robyn: That was important. That group accountability and ongoing support.

Karen: They identified strengths in themselves and reinforced that for the others. They were open and honest with each another.

As our conversation explained, the FYI Program was established to support first-year pre-service educators who identified themselves as 'at risk' in the university context. Although our use of the model of critical reflection (Macfarlane et al., 2006) was not new, its use in the FYI Program enabled us to learn how the model could be employed by students on a daily basis. The model provided a framework that the students could use to problem-solve the difficulties that they were experiencing. The students learnt to use the model independently. They deconstructed and confronted particular problems and, in searching for strategies that would be useful, they demonstrated their attempts to theorise and think otherwise.

In doing this, the students started to demonstrate that they were drawing on the strengths that they had developed in their lives outside the university. Yet, at the same time, they were beginning to hone their academic skills and to take on the Discourse (Gee, 1996) of 'being' a university student. Gee (1996) highlighted that becoming an 'insider' of a particular Discourse requires learning the 'right' combination of 'putting words, deeds, values, other people, and things together in integral combinations for specific times and places' (p. viii). As we explained elsewhere (see Noble & Henderson, 2008), 'the students were able to achieve the "doing-saying combination" (Gee, 1996, p. viii) without the angst that they had felt initially' (p. 14). In other words, as the students were learning the Discourse, they were being inducted into the university context.

Building a pedagogy of induction: Education Commons (Project 1)

Robyn: If we leave the FYI Program and consider Education Commons, it is really that project that illustrates how a pedagogy of induction can work.

Karen: True. Induction into the teaching profession was certainly our starting point for Education Commons. We set out with the idea that induction into the profession at the beginning of Education study could be a way of helping pre-service educators build a teacher identity. And, of course, we wanted to address the issue of teachers leaving the profession early in their career.

Robyn: Education Commons really made us think about how we might enable pre-service educators, even those early in their study, to take up the Discourse of being a teacher.

Karen: That's right. Being able to think, talk and act like a teacher in a supportive environment was crucial to the project.

Robyn: If you think about Gee's notion of an affinity space, Education Commons does that well. It brings together a group of people with a common interest in the topic, including experienced and novice teachers, principals and sometimes academics – for the panel. Then in the audience we have pre-service educators along with teachers from schools and academics.

DOI: 10.1057/9781137473028.0005

Karen: Yes. Novices and experts together, discussing an educational issue. It's a simple concept, but it does work.

Robyn: And it really allows for multiple perspectives to be heard.

Karen: Yes it does. I think it's imperative that pre-service educators hear teachers talking and sharing diverse opinions about how to go about particular teaching tasks.

Robyn: I agree. It is imperative that pre-service educators hear the different ways that educational problems can be approached. We certainly don't want them to think that teaching amounts to a one-size-fits-all approach.

Karen: It seems, too, that hearing teachers is also useful for learning how they think about particular topics, how they talk about those topics, the dilemmas they experience, and so on.

Robyn: That's what the induction is about, isn't it? And it comes back to Gee's work on Discourses – knowing how to think, talk, act, believe, value, like a teacher.

Karen: But we are not talking about teachers all talking the same way or thinking the same way or doing the same thing. Having repertoires of practice is really important.

Robyn: Kalantzis and Cope talked about how teachers need to develop a repertoire of practice. I find their definition really useful. They say a repertoire of practice is the sum of a whole range of things – strategies, ways of working, know-how and so on. In developing those, a teacher is building a tool kit – but it's more than that.

Karen: Definitely. Isn't it about being about to weave together those things and to be able to find a way of working through the complexities?

Robyn: Let me look up their website for exactly what they say. ... Here it is on their 'New Learning' website. They say: 'An expansive and expanding repertoire of practice provides the foundation for sophisticated professional endeavour and professional connoisseurship – it provides for deliberate and thoughtful choice.'

Karen: Not a technicist approach.

Robyn: Certainly not. Transformative rather than technicist.

DOI: 10.1057/9781137473028.0005

Karen: And that's where the model of critical reflection works so
           well. The complexities can be teased out and issues identified
           through the deconstruct and confront stages. The theorise
           stage means that lots of thinking has to happen, to search
           for solutions to a problem and to articulate why particular
           approaches might work. And, of course, the think otherwise
           stage is about seeing that there are usually multiple ways of
           working or enacting a solution.

Robyn: The model of critical reflection really does support a peda-
           gogy of induction.

Karen: It offers a way of taking up the Discourse of being a teacher
           and thinking, acting and talking like a teacher in a context
           with novices and experts. It's helping to build a professional
           identity.

Robyn: Yet, it also allows for individual variations of Discourse. It
           allows for the dynamic, fluid nature of identity and for a
           troubling of taken-for-granted ideas and assumptions.

It was through the Education Commons project that we have been
able to illustrate how a pedagogy of induction works. It involves experts
and novices coming together in what Gee (2004) called an affinity space.
In that space, educational issues are discussed using a framework of critical reflection. As a result of those discussions, the issue or problem is
unpacked, research is conducted to explore and theorise, and multiple
suggestions are made in order to think otherwise about the issue or to
suggest multiple solutions to a problem. In doing this, the participants
are drawing on appropriate discourses and building both personal and
professional identities.

Extending into new contexts: Projects 2, 4 and 5

Through conducting the FYI Program and Education Commons, we
learnt about processes that enabled deep and critical discussion and
reflection. The model of critical reflection (Macfarlane et al., 2006)
provided us with a framework to shape discussions, as well as to examine our own practice. Our experiences suggested that we could extend
the processes into other contexts and we decided to try to do that. In
particular, we used the processes in three additional projects: Education

Commons International (Project 2), the extension of Education Commons into a school context (Project 4) and Doc Chat (Project 5). Each of these projects was described in Chapter 1.

Karen: It's interesting how our practice has changed over time. We are much more relaxed now about not over-preparing for Education Commons discussions.

Robyn: Yes, that's certainly the case. Think back to the first Education Commons. We were so prepared! We even wrote questions that the audience could ask and taped them under the chairs in the room. We were so worried that the conversation wouldn't flow and that there would be no interaction or silences. We were insuring ourselves against failure of the process.

Karen: That was silly, wasn't it? We talk about pre-service educators bringing strengths, their skills and knowledges from their lives outside the university, to their study. Yet, on that occasion we seemed to forget that.

Robyn: I know. Now we never worry. We know that the conversation will happen and that we can guide the conversation around the stages of the model of critical reflection.

Karen: If there was deadly silence, one of us would ask a question or throw in an idea.

Robyn: Of course. And we've seen students develop in that respect too.

Karen: And other participants.

Robyn: I think we've developed as well. We don't guide the conversation as much as we used to.

Karen: No, we don't.

Robyn: It really has been the process that we've used for Education Commons that has proved so successful. Using critical reflection to frame discussions is a significant aspect of the process. And letting the participants determine where the conversation goes is so important.

Karen: That's an essential part of professional learning really.

Robyn: Yes. And we've been able to extend Education Commons and to show that the process works in other contexts.

DOI: 10.1057/9781137473028.0005

Karen: I guess we always expected that Education Commons International would work as Education Commons did.

Robyn: We did. When you think about it, the main difference between Education Commons and Education Commons International is that everyone involved in Education Commons is in the same room, while Education Commons International operates with half the panel and half the audience in Australia and the rest in the USA.

Karen: The process is the same, but we had to rely on technology to link the two groups of people.

Robyn: The video link always worked well, fortunately.

Karen: The good thing about Education Commons International was that it expanded the multiple perspectives with an international flavour and that was really appreciated by the audience.

Robyn: Yes. Members of the audience commented on the similarities that presented. They seemed surprised about that.

Karen: I think the professional learning aspect has been an important learning for us. When we began Education Commons, we didn't think too much about the possibility that there would be benefits for those who attended as panel members. I thought that it was going to be our pre-service educators who would benefit. And they did, of course. But the teachers who participated, both novice and experienced, kept reporting that Education Commons was a great source of professional learning for them as well.

Robyn: That has been a consistent response from those who have participated.

It seems to me that teachers really like having an involvement in these conversations about teaching.

Karen: Yes, some have been novices – novice teachers as well as our pre-service educators. Others have been very experienced teachers.

A clear outcome of the Education Commons format was that all participants saw it as a form of professional learning. Attendance was voluntary and, apart from the decisions we made about choice of topic – and we

DOI: 10.1057/9781137473028.0005

always tried to have current topics that would have general appeal with members of the teaching profession – the conversations were not pre-planned. Where the conversation went and the terrain it covered were totally dependent on the input of participants.

Education Commons operated as an affinity space (Gee, 2004). Novices and experts interacted in the same space, discussing issues and ideas that were part of their shared interests. The 'space' was slightly different in the different programs, as already discussed, because Education Commons (Project 1) operated within a single room and Education Commons International (Project 2) connected rooms in different countries. The video connection provided synchronous discussion which was mediated by technology. As was discussed earlier in this chapter, affinity spaces bring together people with 'common interests, endeavours, goals, or practices' (Gee, 2004, p. 85) and the interactions that occur offer opportunities for learning. It was evident that learning occurred as participants shared their experiences, asked questions, compared ideas and practices, and so on.

In the extension into a school context (Project 4) and Doc Chat (Project 5), the intent had to be different from Education Commons as the projects were not part of initial teacher education. We needed to consider the contexts and the participants. Project 4 involved teachers in approximately 15 schools and the focus was professional learning about literacy education, while Project 5 was a support mechanism for doctoral students. Nevertheless, both projects drew on the concept of an affinity space (Gee, 2004).

Karen: Robyn, you've been the one involved in Doc Chat, so you'll need to explain how that worked.

Robyn: I have to make it clear that I didn't start Doc Chat. It already existed when I took over the role as doctoral programs coordinator.

Karen: But you've played a significant role in Doc Chat since you took over the coordinator role.

Robyn: Yes, that's true. However, I feel as though I do little more than provide the opportunity for an affinity space to exist.

Karen: Like the other projects, it sounds as though it is participants who decide what happens.

DOI: 10.1057/9781137473028.0005

Robyn: That is certainly the case. Doc Chat is a fortnightly meeting of on-campus students who are mostly studying a doctorate in the field of education. We do have some other doctoral students who join us from outside of education. Our meetings are an hour long and we discuss whatever the students want to discuss.

Karen: So what are some examples?

Robyn: They are mostly aspects of doctoral study, but the discussion topics go well beyond those. The group is diverse. The students are an international group; many of them are living temporarily in Australia while they complete their doctoral study. Others are Australian students. They vary in age, gender, and of course they are all at different stages of doctoral study. Some have just started and others are close to completion.

Karen: That sounds like an affinity space with novices and experts in the same space. And they all have a common endeavour and goal.

Robyn: I suppose I fit into the 'expert', but I learn as much as the students do.

Karen: Why's that?

Robyn: If we go back to the model of critical reflection and think about multiple perspectives, everyone at Doc Chat brings experience to the discussions. The students are reading relevant literature with different theoretical lenses. They bring different cultural backgrounds and different life experiences. Once you start getting that group theorising and thinking otherwise, the potential for multiple perspectives is enormous.

Karen: In some ways, that sounds a little like Education Commons International.

Robyn: Except that the common endeavour in Doc Chat is very broad. The commonalities are their interest in methodologies, theories, literature review, the things that doctoral students are engaged with. Some of the discussions have been about specialised knowledge. While doctoral students are specialising in different areas of knowledge, they can contribute to discussions from different perspectives. However, one of my learnings has been about cultural taken-for-granteds.

DOI: 10.1057/9781137473028.0005

Karen: For example?

Robyn: One example is about who can produce knowledge. Some of the doctoral students have discussed whether they should question and challenge their supervisors' thinking. Such discussions have prompted much thinking about the cultural assumptions we make and that has led to some interesting discussion about culture and study more generally.

Karen: That's almost a different type of knowledge, isn't it?

The discussion about Doc Chat highlighted the importance to doctoral students of what Gee (2004) referred to as intensive and extensive knowledge. The former is specialised knowledge while the latter is broader and less specialised. It was evident that the affinity space (Gee, 2004) offered by Doc Chat enabled learning of those two types of knowledge. In some cases, the discussion and learning related directly to doctoral study, but at other times students wanted to learn how to negotiate the everyday elements of being a doctoral student in Australia.

In some ways, this was similar to the situation in the FYI Program, where students often wanted to talk about and deal with barriers to study. Sometimes the barriers were a part of daily life, such as having somewhere to live or managing family emergencies. At other times, though, the students were concerned about specific academic aspects of being a student. What was apparent in each of the projects was that an affinity space (Gee, 2004) brought together people with similar interests and promoted discussion that focused on the personal and professional (for example, as part of Projects 1, 2 and 4) or personal and academic (as part of Projects 3 and 5).

Conclusion

In this chapter, we discussed the tenets that underpinned the five teaching–learning projects that were part of our research on a pedagogy of induction, and we described the model of critical reflection (Macfarlane et al., 2006) that was employed within the projects and as a research tool. Through a reflective research conversation, we teased out how the tenets

DOI: 10.1057/9781137473028.0005

worked in practice as well as some of the insights that became obvious to us as researchers. In doing so, we highlighted:

▸ the utility of critical reflection to deconstruct current practice and to reconstruct future practice;
▸ the value of discussion in critical reflection;
▸ the positive effects of collaborative critical reflection;
▸ the way that learners' strengths can be brought to new contexts and learning;
▸ the importance of learning a new Discourse as part of professional induction;
▸ the potential for transformative learning.

If we consider the implications for teacher education, then some salient points become obvious. Firstly, a pedagogy of induction encourages multiple perspectives rather than one-size-fits-all solutions to educational issues. If we want to develop teachers who can cope with the ongoing changes that continue to be experienced in education, then it is important to consider repertoires of practice (Kalantzis & Cope, n.d.). Secondly, a pedagogy of induction works well in the spaces between conventional course structures. Providing opportunities for critical reflection in a safe space where peers, novices and experts can interact, would seem to be important.

DOI: 10.1057/9781137473028.0005

3
Using Place and Space to Deconstruct and Confront

Abstract: *This chapter uses two stages of a model of critical reflection to deconstruct and confront aspects of a pedagogy of induction. Drawing on longitudinal research, the analysis deconstructs notions of teacher and teaching through shared experiences and problematises the main tenets of knowledge and practice that have become normalised within the teaching profession. The human geography notion of spatial imaginaries, focusing on space and place, provides insights into how research participants deconstruct collaborative learning experiences which were designed to enable learning, build professional identity and inform new ways of preparing and supporting those belonging to, or about to join, the teaching profession.*

Keywords: critical reflection; deconstruction; normalisation; pedagogy of induction; professional identity; spatial imaginaries

Henderson, Robyn and Karen Noble. *Professional Learning, Induction and Critical Reflection: Building Workforce Capacity in Education.* Basingstoke: Palgrave Macmillan, 2015. DOI: 10.1057/9781137473028.0006.

Introduction

In this chapter and the two that follow, we explain a pedagogy of induction and its place in induction and professional learning in education. We use the model of critical reflection (Macfarlane et al., 2006) that we used throughout the overall research project to frame these chapters. This chapter focuses specifically on the first two stages of the model – deconstruct and confront. Our main purpose is to tease out what we mean by a pedagogy of induction. In using the first stage – deconstruct – of Macfarlane et al.'s (2006) model, we set out to explore:

▸ What are we doing and how are we doing it?
▸ How did a pedagogy of induction 'work'?
▸ What is working successfully and what isn't?
▸ What might we need to explore further?

The second stage – confront – is generally a reflection on what is working and what is not working, with the aim of identifying a particular aspect for further consideration and development. In our publication with Cross (2013), we teased out some questions for the confront stage:

▸ What is working? What is not working?
▸ What might I need to change?
▸ Has a specific focus for further consideration been identified?
▸ Have weaknesses or areas for change been considered?
▸ Has a problem or issue been identified?
▸ Has there been a decision that an aspect of practice needs to be modified or changed? (from Henderson et al., 2013, p. 51).

During the course of our projects, the confront stage was important in the design-based research approach (Barab & Squire, 2004; The Design-Based Research Collective, 2003; Wang & Hannafin, 2005) that we employed. Indeed, our critical reflection on the practice of the projects and on the research being conducted was instrumental in modifying our practice during the projects. However, in terms of this book, we considered the confront stage before we began to write. In other words, we had already decided on what we should deconstruct. Although we have embedded the confront stage in this chapter along with the deconstruct stage, in one sense we have changed the order of the two stages. We will return to this point in Chapter 6.

DOI: 10.1057/9781137473028.0006

The emergent and evolving design-based research approach that we used in conducting the five projects – Education Commons (Project 1), Education Commons International (Project 2), the FYI Program (Project 3), Extending Education Commons into a school context (Project 4) and Doc Chat (Project 5) – has contributed to understandings about induction, professional learning, career development, critical reflection and workforce capacity. In this chapter, we use the lens of spatial imaginaries (Gruenewald, 2003) to deconstruct some aspects of a pedagogy of induction. As Gruenewald (2003) explained, the study of space provides opportunities to understand 'the nature of our relationships with each other and the world' (p. 622).

Collaborative deconstruction

When we began Project 1, Education Commons, we argued that pre-service educators need to be provided with opportunities, from the outset of their Education study, to develop the knowledge and skills for shaping high quality practice and increased professional effectiveness. We thought that the development of the skills of critical reflection, individually and in collaboration with others, would lay the foundations for understanding and explaining what it means to 'teach' and how one constructs oneself as 'teacher' within the complex social contexts of teaching. Our focus across all of the projects has been on understanding action, but at the same time working to create action – to disrupt grand narratives and taken-for-granted truths to create new, transformative ways of being, knowing and doing. In the case of Education Commons and Education Commons International, being, knowing and doing related to teaching. We wanted to disrupt the status quo through these projects, trying to move beyond one-size-fits-all approaches to teaching. At the same time, we wanted to create conditions for reimagining new ways of doing, being and knowing teaching (Gee, 1996; Ryan, 2012). This required a focus on processes and outcomes.

In line with Schön's (1983) seminal work, a central part of our task was to explicate insights, values and strategies that effective teachers bring to situations that they encounter in practice. Our challenge was to do so in ways that capture a theory-in/of/for-action perspective that accounts for multiple perspectives and contexts. Therefore, within each of the projects we have privileged process to build the complex capabilities that are

DOI: 10.1057/9781137473028.0006

necessary for teaching. We have thus worked to ensure that pre-service educators have ways of conceptualising and evaluating possible courses of action across their teaching careers. That is, we want them to 'know what to do when they don't know what to do.'

One of the characteristics of two of the projects – Education Commons and Education Commons International – was that we were working to deconstruct notions of teacher and teaching through shared experiences. This lead to pulling apart or teasing out the main tenets of knowledge and practice that have become normalised in the context of the profession. Our position was that, although individuals can engage in critical reflection, it is through collaborative endeavours that multiple perspectives become particularly evident. The highlighting of multiple perspectives can help to expand repertoires of knowledge, experiences and practices (Kalantzis & Cope, n.d.). This then leads to the construction of new ways of being, knowing and doing that are not delimiting because they are informed by multiple perspectives. They are therefore more likely to be transformative in nature (Henderson et al., 2013).

Spatial imaginaries

The human geography notion of spatial imaginaries (Gruenewald, 2003) provides a means by which we are able to gain a better understanding of how the participants in the projects deconstructed collaborative learning experiences. Along with looking at their concomitant 'sense of place' (Gruenewald, 2003; Holloway & Hubbard, 2001), this has been an essential process within our research. It also provides us with insights into how a pedagogy of induction enables learning, builds professional identity, supports existing ways of being, knowing and doing, and informs new ways of preparing and supporting those within a profession. Three of our projects – Education Commons, Education Commons International and the extension of Education Commons into a school context – related particularly to teaching. The other two projects had different foci, but the intention of those projects was similar. The FYI Program was about inducting new university students into the university context, while Doc Chat focused on academic life.

The spatial imaginaries of human geography have also been useful because of our conceptualisation of our projects in terms of affinity spaces (Gee, 2004). Not only have we talked about the place or space where participants with 'common interests, endeavours, goals, or practices' (Gee, 2004, p. 85) come together, we have also recognised that all of the participants in our projects are professionally situated. Participants work and learn within particular places and contexts. As Bartholomaeus (2013) explained when talking about school use of place-based education, a concern with place enables students (or, in our projects, participants) to 'understand how their community has been shaped, to recognise the resources available in their community, and identify ways they can contribute to its future development' (p. 18).

In Chapter 2, we identified learners' strengths as important to the way our projects worked. Many of the strengths of participants came from their lives outside the university context. A concern with place, then, helps to 'keep alive a connection' (Gruenewald, 2003, p. 620) with other parts of participants' lives, the experiences they have had, and the skills they have learnt. Additionally, the way that our projects drew on problems of practice or real life problems from the profession reinforced the importance of place.

In human geography and in educational research, imaginative geographies and geographical imaginations are not new ideas (Hargreaves, 1994; Lowenthal, 1961; Wright, 1947). In fact, these frameworks have been applied in a variety of contexts with the aim of enhancing understandings about physical and tangible aspects of life experience. In Education Commons and Education Commons International, the emphasis was on the imaginaries, or the imagined realities of participants in terms of their understandings about agency, power, either overt or covert, and an emerging sense of place as they navigated their membership of the teaching profession and engaged in professional learning.

In this sense, then, we understand space as socially produced with the interconnectedness of participants' notions of space and place establishing a spatial dialectic (Lehtovuori, 2005). As Gruenewald (2003) explained, an understanding of space, place or social context is key to making sense of relationships and of our experiences. Place-based consciousness is understood to be pedagogical in nature, because it helps us understand 'who, what, and where we are, as well as how we might live our lives' (Gruenewald, 2003, p. 636). This means that the geographical imaginaries that are conveyed need to be understood as multidimensional. They are not only descriptions of how participants understood their involvement in a learning community, but they also

DOI: 10.1057/9781137473028.0006

show how they were constructing space and place to find ways of changing or reimagining their experiences. This view provides insights into how participants were seeing themselves in terms of their profession. It was apparent as we worked through each of the projects that exploration by way of spatial imaginaries would prove a useful means of teasing out the multiplicity and depth of perceived benefit of the social support emerging through the projects' affinity spaces (Gee, 2004). We were interested in the ways that participants negotiated the multiple aspects of their lived experiences.

Gruenewald's (2003) five dimensions of place – perceptual, sociological, ideological, political and ecological – helped to provide an exploration of the ways in which participants in each of the learning communities deconstructed their lived experiences. As Gruenewald highlighted, a focus on place is important, because 'places *make* us: As occupants of particular places with particular attributes, our identity and our possibilities are shaped' (p. 621). In particular, insights about place offer ways of understanding how the projects impacted on participants' sense of self, their professional identity and their professional learning. These insights can illustrate the depth of understanding that developed through the process of reflection on experiences and learnings within the communities. Gruenewald's dimensions draw on a multidisciplinary base and this complements our argument for multiple perspectives and seeing the world and our place within it from different perspectives.

A perceptual dimension of place

If we look at a perceptual dimension of place, a central focus in some of our projects was pre-service educators' perceived understandings of their induction into the teaching profession. Although the physical environment of a learning community sometimes seems inanimate, as a place to be inhabited at particular times, it became evident that participants' reactions and responses to their participation in the contexts of the FYI Program, Education Commons and Education Commons International were significant indicators of the projects' successes. Each participant brought different experiences, prior understandings and funds of knowledge (Gonzales et al., 2005b) to the projects, as well as their own communication and ways of participating in the social world of the projects. This meant that the ways in which participants were able to effectively deconstruct their induction to the profession and relate that

DOI: 10.1057/9781137473028.0006

to other aspects of their lived experience were important. The following excerpt from the FYI Program narratives illustrates this point:

> I think that each one of us values one another. Well, it has certainly felt like that for me. I now think that I have knowledge that is worth sharing and that I don't just have to follow what someone else has done ... You get to look at your strengths and the small steps that you are taking are a focus ... that is a really important thing; that is empowerment just in itself. When we talk about our stuff and we listen to others talking about their own issues, you come to realise that you are not alone and that, even though you think you are lost, you can actually do something so small like suggest meeting somewhere, just to walk in together. It is the little things that we can all do that can make a difference to how someone feels about coming back time and time again and getting to feel comfortable here at uni. Well, that's how it is for me. It's always easier to get used to difficult situations if you feel as though you have support and you're not on your own. Mind you, I have always had a friend to do things with before. It has been scary being here on my own and having to start from scratch. It felt really bad in the beginning, but now you don't really even think about it. You just know it will be okay and that the group is here to support you however you need ... I guess now it just feels like you are more a part of it ... You feel as though in a sense, you belong here and have earned the right to be here. (FYI Program: Pre-service educator)

In this excerpt, the pre-service educator's focus was on developing a strong social network within the learning community. While skills of friendship were transferable from other contexts, she highlighted how she needed strategies to assist her to deal with the emotional response to the unfamiliar context of the university. The focus in the FYI Program was on becoming a university student, but that would seem to be the first step in her journey, as pre-service educator, towards becoming a teacher. Induction, then, is seen as a fluid movement towards knowing and being a university student initially, then later as a pre-service educator working towards joining the teaching profession. At this first stage, initial survival was understood, in the pre-service educator's words, as a 'rite of passage'.

The pre-service educator's perception of the context shaped and formed the ways in which her participation and her communications with others were able to occur. As she explained, the focus on what they know and their perceived feelings and attitudes towards adjustment to their new environment helped to heighten their awareness of how to deal with spatial aspects of their learning experiences. She wanted to feel as if she belonged and she wanted to feel comfortable in the university context.

DOI: 10.1057/9781137473028.0006

Education Commons operated differently from the FYI Program in that it deliberately created an affinity space (Gee, 1996; Henderson & Hirst, 2007) where pre-service educators, novice teachers and experienced teachers were able to meet. Participants acknowledged that their experiences in this learning community were of significant benefit, regardless of their experience in the teaching profession. There was recognition that the ability to perceive the learning community as a place for all to learn could work to deregulate traditional models of professional development. Although novice and experienced teachers were invited to participate in the learning community for the benefit of pre-service educators, it became apparent that experienced educators regarded participation in the learning community as important to their own professional learning. For example:

> I really love listening to the stories of other people. I think no matter what your context you always learn something. No matter how many years of experience you learn something. What's been really an eye opener is actually listening to some of the first year experiences and realising that I'm still learning from people who are in their first year and I think that's a really valuable understanding for me, that you never stop learning. (Education Commons: Experienced teacher participant)

Such data speak to notions of renewal and, accountability rejuvenation that can occur in professional learning. This foregrounds the potential of a pedagogy of induction for developing career optimism, whereby those new to the profession as well as those who have been in the profession for a considerable period of time perceive benefits in participating. Similarly, examples such as those evident in the transcripts reinforce the need to focus on the philosophical standpoint of teacher and teaching, rather than merely being focused on teaching practice. Current policies privilege regulation and performativity measures. As Hardy (2013) pointed out, the increasing centralisation of education within Australia 'necessarily abstracts from, and marginalises, the specific' (p. 68). In contrast, the perceptions of professional learning that focus on the specific, as seen in the transcripts just discussed, help to establish belonging and to encourage the sharing of knowledge, skills and experiences.

A sociological dimension of place

A sociological dimension of place evokes person–place relationships. From this perspective, it is interesting to view the ways in which

DOI: 10.1057/9781137473028.0006

participants construct the physical space of a learning community. In interviews about the FYI Program, some of the participants talked about the learning community as providing 'a sanctuary' or 'a place to escape' (see Henderson & Noble, 2013). These understandings of place were different from the assessable coursework environments that they were experiencing in the university context. Some of the pre-service educators regarded the assessment situation as one that was high stakes. They viewed their first foray into university as their only chance. If they were unsuccessful, then they could not see that they could remain or try again later.

Feedback from participants of all of the programs involving pre-service educators (Projects 1, 2 and 3) and the doctoral students (Project 5) indicated that creating a physical space within the university to meet – whether that be an informal space like the refectory, in the case of Doc Chat, or a more formal teaching space – was not as important as the purposes and goals the space could help them achieve. For example, the pre-service educators who participated in the FYI Program argued that the space enabled them to explore the complexities of the teaching profession. They regarded the meeting room as a safe space where they did not have to perform in ways that were expected of them in other places within the university, such as tutorials and workshops. As one pre-service educator explained:

> Being able to come here and know that this space is ours for two hours, that it is just us... coming together to see how we are all going, to take care of each other and to check up on how we are all going along. I know that each week when we open the door again and go back out to the "uni world" that it is only a week at a time. In the beginning just getting through a week at a time was a challenge. (FYI Program: Pre-service educator)

So while the physical space may not have changed, it was the informal arrangement of the learning communities that was regarded as a noteworthy characteristic. The relationships with others attending the FYI Program were identified as playing a significant role, and the social space where those relationships were able to develop occurred in a space between traditional course enrolments.

Deconstructing the learning communities in terms of the sociological dimension requires the adoption of a view that 'places are what people make of them' (Gruenewald, 2003, p. 627). In other words, the learning community is evolutionary and it is how the person–place relationships emerge and develop over time that mediates the meaning making for participants. Throughout the voluminous narrative data that we collected over time, it is apparent that the participants of the projects found the various learning communities to be places of connection. They not only connected with others with common interests (Gee, 1996), but they were able to make connections between their experiences in other contexts and the professional identity that they were developing. For example, one of the beginning teachers involved in the Education Commons project was able to deconstruct her understandings gained from hearing the experiences of others, together with the application of her knowledge and understandings gained through her sustained membership of the learning community. She was also able to apply these in her own school context. She demonstrated that it was about 'knowing what to do when you don't know what to do':

> When you first start coming [to Education Commons] it is overwhelming. But all I can say is stick it out because my first term [as a teacher] is proof of being able to be a better professional ... global educator because I've just been put in the middle of nowhere and have had to survive. It's only through discussion with the people that come in and see you on a panel, that I've been able to go through my notes and the discussions and skills that I've acquired through Education Commons, that I've been able to deal with the many, many challenges I've had in my first term. For a first year, first term I feel on top of the world, I love teaching. I haven't been turned away yet and I do take a huge part of that as being, participating in Education Commons. When I am facing challenges it is the model of critical reflection that helps me work it through ... It is a great thing to come to – when the other beginning teachers and I talk. They don't have this – I am trying to teach them the model of critical reflection to help them now. (Education Commons: Novice teacher participant)

What is also apparent here is that this novice teacher was able to deconstruct the challenges that she was facing in her school context through the use of the model of critical reflection. Additionally, she was attempting to support others in a similar situation through the application of the model of critical reflection in a collaborative way. The model was being used to traverse unfamiliar terrain, both individually and collectively. Those involved were drawing on their various funds of knowledge (Gonzales et al., 2005b) to collaboratively make sense of their new place in their community, school and classrooms.

While pre-service educators and novice teachers find value in the Education Commons learning community, it is also apparent that, when experienced teachers are asked to deconstruct their experiences

DOI: 10.1057/9781137473028.0006

of participating in this context, there are perceived benefits for them in relation to their own professional understandings. For example:

> We don't have that opportunity very often, to be able to talk to our future teachers, to be able to say look, this is so important. This is something that you need to have ... absolutely fundamental. If they don't have this then they don't have everything else. So just to be able to share that with them I think that was really important. As an experienced teacher I take away from it too – not only being able to help those entering the profession but also learning from the reflections and experiences of others – it is invaluable. We can all explore together what is important to us in teacher education rather than only focusing on departmental priorities. (Education Commons: Experienced teacher panellist)

Just as the novice teacher was able to do, the experienced teacher panellist was able to see broader application of the process of Education Commons to growing the profession. As the teacher explained, professional learning could occur through the sharing of experiences and reflections on those experiences. Similar ideas came from academic participants in Education Commons. For example:

> I guess what I bring to Education Commons is yet again a different perspective, a different point of view. Certainly having been a curriculum coordinator working with teachers on professional development before coming into university life, I try and bring those perspectives. Also the perspectives of somebody who has worked in different states because not only are there the different concepts within Queensland itself but all the different ways of looking at education and the ways that schools have been working in different states of Australia. (Education Commons: Academic panellist)

These participants in Education Commons' panels seemed to be saying that the interactions and relationships that were first formed in the learning communities were valuable and valued. Participation also offered the opportunity to extend beyond the immediate context of Education Commons. Pre-service educators were connected with experienced teachers. They were also connecting with academics beyond the formal curriculum of their university study. For example, one academic participant said:

> I have heard after Education Commons students talking in the corridors about some of those experiences so certainly although I may not have the feedback myself I can actually engage with the students and what they've actually received out of those sessions. (Education Commons: Academic participant)

DOI: 10.1057/9781137473028.0006

These interview excerpts suggested that there were particular ideas that were repeated across many of the narratives. In deconstructing their experiences in the FYI Program and Education Commons, participants in the projects identified the usefulness of opportunities to explore their understandings and experiences informally with others and to share a range of experiences. An experienced teacher who participated in Education Commons explained:

> I certainly think the benefit of sharing experience. I vividly remember the second Education Commons. There were a lot of young, pre-graduate teachers who, I got the impression, really got a lot out of the experience ... they were learning from a group of people who'd been around for a little bit. They were eager to continue the conversations after the event too. That gave them another opportunity to engage in a different way with professional conversation. Also the other way that I feel for some of us who were there, that we benefitted a lot from listening to each other. Networking as well, the opportunity to meet people who work in education in the local area who I hadn't met previously. It was good to meet those people. (Education Commons: Experienced teacher panellist)

Likewise, pre-service educators highlighted the importance of spaces and places where they could explore ways of being a teacher in an informal, non-assessable context. One pre-service educator said:

> There was a lady from a fairly large girls' school in town who's in a senior position, so it allowed me to meet that lady and to share some of the challenges that we're both facing. So I think probably in the down time afterwards, when we were having a cup of coffee and a talk, I found that really worthwhile. You don't do this in coursework – it is always about assessment. You are not judged in Education Commons in the same way. (Education Commons: Pre-service educator participant)

In deconstructing learning experiences from Education Commons and teasing out the key ways that learning seemed to be occurring, it was evident that many participants identified ways of learning that were different from the established ways of learning in the university context. The importance of interactions and relationships was also highlighted, as was the need to find ways to form connections between the different courses that students studied. A pre-service educator explained:

> With Education Commons there's the panel and then the pedagogical conversation ... the pedagogical conversation away from the panel is always fantastic ... [the academics are] definitely an inspiration and a highlight in bringing,

DOI: 10.1057/9781137473028.0006

connecting it to our university and how as pre-service teachers we can start dealing with some of the issues that are presented in Education Commons. So, and I guess you can't really pick, each issue has its, each has experts in it and so each of them are all very valuable. So I don't think there's one specific topic or person that stood out because the reason they have Education Commons is to have all those specific issues. (Education Commons: Pre-service educator participant)

The experienced teacher panellists also discussed the importance of privileging interactions and creating the space for professional relationships to develop. Some said that:

I found the Education Commons a really worthwhile experience. I'm somebody that loves to share my experiences in the teaching profession. I also think that it helps for the pre-service teachers who are currently undergoing studies to hear some real-world examples. In the Education Commons that I was in they actually did hear about some of the aspects that didn't go quite so well for people in their teaching career and what led to some people leaving their teaching career and pursuing other careers. (Education Commons: Experienced teacher panellist)

About having, getting, a really realistic view of the teaching profession, that is one of the big benefits of Education Commons. I really do because I know when I went through my teaching degree at uni you never really got to see the full picture of exactly what pressures the classroom teacher or any teacher is under. It would have helped to have known that from the start, to be better prepared for reality. (Education Commons: Experienced teacher panellist)

Participants across the learning communities were able to deconstruct the ways in which their membership was understood as an investment in place. In Education Commons and Education Commons International, participants referred to their place within the teaching profession – both real and imagined. They were able to articulate the value of the person–place relationships that developed and matured over time, as well as to highlight the connection between participation in the learning community and their own sense of career optimism.

An ideological dimension of place

Within an ideological dimension, spaces and places can be seen as expressions of relationships of power, domination and ideologies (Gruenewald, 2003). From this perspective, learning communities can be analysed in terms of social formation. As Gruenewald (2003) highlighted, an examination of this dimension of place considers the ways in which the space 'reflects and reproduces social relationships of power and domination' (p. 628). In many ways, the learning communities that were developed as part of the teaching–learning projects challenged participants' pre-existing understandings of interpersonal and professional relationships, especially in relation to power dynamics.

As an example, participants in the FYI Program (Project 3) repeatedly commented on the impact of having a supportive environment within the university context. They explained the program as a place where they felt that they could escape from the perceived pressures of the formal aspects of their study and where they could engage in constructive, critically reflective processes each week. The next interview excerpt illustrates that the participant saw the power dynamic shifting considerably and this resulted in thinking about the academic facilitators in a different way.

> That was really good because in those meetings I got to realise that, yes, they are academics but, yes, they are real people as well. They can relate on the academic level when they have to, but they can also bring it down to our level and help bring us up to the academic level. So it was sort of, okay, I don't know what to expect, they're academics, they're going to bring different terminologies, different everything else, but they're real people. They have a life, they have families, they're real people who've been there done that. (FYI Program: Pre-service educator)

As a collective, the pre-service educators who participated in the FYI Program co-constructed narratives about their experiences, often using metaphor as a way of explaining what they had experienced. In many of their narratives, they referred to the door of the room that was the regular weekly meeting place. Shutting the door to begin the session seemed to have a particular significance to all of them. As one explained:

> I make sure that no matter what else is happening, I am always here on a Wednesday. Sometimes it is the only sane time that I have. [Names of the academics] are always so happy to see us and they seem to really care about how we are going. Our group has really become a bit like a big family. We all listen and we all share and help each other out. No-one is really in control and we just all help each other out. [Names of the academics] made sure we all got our turn in the beginning, that we were all included, but we do that for ourselves now. We organise ourselves. If they [the academics] are running late, we just get started and everyone joins in as they arrive. It's great. I don't know what I would do without them all now. (FYI Program: Pre-service educator)

DOI: 10.1057/9781137473028.0006

The relationships built by the pre-service educators who engaged in the FYI Program seemed to break down some of the power structures that the pre-service educators had thought existed in the university context. The establishment of a specific time and place for students to meet informally and regularly enabled the students to become independent and at the same time interdependent. They were building skills as individuals, but they were also building relationships that enabled them to do much more than they could as individuals. It was evident that the social relationships of power shifted over time, with the place and space of the learning communities developing both individual and collective responsibility. According to one participant:

> So when you know, a bit like when you're teaching, you talk about process and you talk about content and if you've got a transformational approach to learning and teaching, it's the process. It's the journey that you're taking us on ... I think because it is like left open, that you don't have any set particular things that you're going to talk about. It's run off the needs of the audience, so like if you've got first to fourth year students and teachers too in the audience you're going to have a conversation that is to their needs basis and that builds on their personal experiences and current struggles or issues. Everyone can learn something from being there and everyone has something to teach others too. Even if you are the first year, you can challenge people to think differently by asking a question or just sharing an experience you have had at school perhaps. (Education Commons: Pre-service educator)

Over time, the participants in the learning communities saw that the emphasis on the structured process, rather than carefully scaffolded content, enabled a more democratic context to emerge. The context was a strongly transformative one, where the space or place was shaped through the expression of ideologies and an understanding of more equal power relationships. One pre-service educator, when talking about Education Commons, highlighted the way that the discussion and critical reflection was helpful for coming to a personal standpoint on particular educational issues. The pre-service educator said:

> And I think that's something that perhaps we haven't explicitly unpacked ... we've learned how you can express your opinion but also how you can receive somebody else's opinion that might be different to yours and critically reflect on it and come to a position of yeah, okay, well that challenges my thinking and therefore my thinking might change as a consequence of it, or well no, that's just further entrenched my perspective. (Education Commons: Pre-service educator)

DOI: 10.1057/9781137473028.0006

A political dimension of place

A political dimension of place is premised by a strong sense of justice and empowerment. It can be understood in terms of power, struggle and resistance and issues around identity and difference (Gruenewald, 2003, p. 631). Each of the projects and the learning communities they established has enabled participants to understand their sense of agency, providing them with opportunities to re-imagine and reshape their identities (see Noble & Henderson, 2008).

Our analysis of the data we have collected in the projects indicates critical steps as pre-service educators move into the university context (FYI Program) and become teachers (Education Commons and Education Commons International). In the FYI Program, the shut door metaphor, that we have already discussed, was used by participants to describe the calm they felt inside the room where the program was conducted. This seemed to be one way that they were able to deal with the disjuncture and discomfort that they felt between their lives inside and outside the university context. In fact, the students' talk about the room and about having to go 'back to the outside world at uni' indicated that they felt like outsiders.

Likewise, across the Education Commons data sets, similar themes emerged where the pre-service educators verbalised their initial struggles to identify with the profession. However, over time they began to visualise their space and place within the professional communities. In doing this, they began to re-vision their own identity and began to feel comfortable participating in the emerging conversations of Education Commons. As Gee (1996) argued, becoming an insider of a particular Discourse requires the 'right ... saying-doing combination' along with appropriate beliefs, values and thinking (p. viii). Over time, the pre-service educators were able to achieve this integration without the angst that they had felt initially. For example, one pre-service educator talked about her initial experiences of Education Commons as feeling like a shy 'marshmallow bunny' who sat quietly and just listened. She explained:

> I think that Education Commons gives confidence. You do have those first and second year marshmallows that can just sit there and just listen and not be threatened to engage ... Well like a sponge, you can take it all in ... and you don't know when you're getting to saturation point but you just sit there and let the water keep running over you just in case there's anything more you can soak up. (Education Commons: Pre-service educator)

DOI: 10.1057/9781137473028.0006

Over the duration of her degree program, however, this pre-service educator developed the confidence to participate in the discussions that were occurring. It became apparent that the 'marshmallow bunny is well and truly gone now…because she's asking for the microphone'. Nevertheless, there was an understanding that everyone was different and that the pre-service educators could choose whether to engage in conversations or to just sit and listen:

> We always want everybody to have an opportunity to speak or to ask a question if they want to, but also for it to be okay not to if you don't want to. (Education Commons: Academic participant)

> So then when they do, like they do develop that confidence because they can just sit there and listen and then as they get further on in their degree they can start being more actively engaged … there is not the pressure to perform until they are comfortable and even then…it is as much as they wish to be active or passive…they choose the level of engagement that they are happy with. (Education Commons: Experienced teacher panellist)

Some pre-service educators also made comparisons to other professional learning contexts that they had experienced. One comparison was with their professional experience placements. For example:

> Where on prac it's a bit more threatening because you are getting assessed and you need to start knowing things and show that you know what you are doing; where Education Commons is more relaxed and more non-threatening and … no expectation…just an opportunity to explore new ideas and challenge yourself. (Education Commons: Pre-service educator)

What is clear is that the politics of identity played out in different ways across different contexts for some of the pre-service educators. There seemed, however, to be a consensus that the learning communities enabled them to feel empowered over time. Through making meaning of interactions and relationships, it was possible for pre-service educators to challenge how they were constructed as learners and as members of the teaching profession. They could achieve a greater awareness of the underlying assumptions driving their actions, and it has been the same for us as design-based researchers and academics. Teaching can empower or oppress, but the processes of critical reflection enabled discovery about the how power works in educational processes (Brookfield, 1995).

DOI: 10.1057/9781137473028.0006

The ecological dimension of place

Rather than thinking globally with regard to transition to university and induction into the teaching profession, the projects sought local solutions to specific issues in context. What is foregrounded in the ecological dimension of place is that there is a need to examine socio-ecological relationships and how the learning communities are the experiential centre of patterns of social domination. To understand the learning journey in this way required an examination of the commitment to the evolution of the learning communities. There was a very limited financial resource required to support each of the learning communities and, furthermore, the spaces used for the learning communities were mostly university classrooms that happened to be empty at that time of the week. Additionally, attendance was always voluntary.

It is obvious from the data that the pre-service educators flourished in the space behind the door (FYI Program), where they likened themselves to squatters occupying a space that was not legitimately theirs in the beginning, and in the other spaces that were established (for example, Education Commons and Education Commons International). Yet, over time, it was evident that their involvement in the learning communities enabled them to come to terms with social injustice issues and their perceptions of marginality. Instead, they were able to identify as agentive and skilful. The pre-service educators were developing as successful lifelong learners and transitioning to become members of the teaching profession. For example:

> I think that without having done Education Commons that I wouldn't be at the stage that I am at now … I'm ready. I don't think I would never have got there, but I do think that it's helped me get there faster. (Education Commons: Graduating pre-service educator)

As the pre-service educators tried to come to terms with the impact of engagement in the learning communities, they compared and contrasted those experiences with other encounters within the professional contexts of teaching, as illustrated in the following excerpt:

> Like at uni you get all that theory and things and you kind of get lost in, well, what does this really mean to teach a class kind of thing? Like it's all well and good … but you ask yourself – How's it relevant? … you sort of get to that point where you're like, what's it useful for? So I think things like Education Commons and we've done a bit of PD as well and that's really helped us really connect back to well, it links with theory, like you've got theory and then

DOI: 10.1057/9781137473028.0006

you've got your professional learning where you get all these new ideas for your own practice... and then you can use it in your prac and things like that. So, Education Commons really helped me build those connections. (Education Commons: Pre-service educator)

Across the different learning communities, an ethics of care (Noddings, 1984) permeated all interactions and relationships. That is, the emphasis was one of collaboration and shared experience, where independence and interdependence were privileged. The person–place relationship was one of valuing diversity. For example:

> I can remember the first sort of ones we came to where, yeah, we weren't saying anything ... it wasn't that I didn't have questions... but it was more of a, I guess you didn't want to say something stupid in front of panel members or teachers. I didn't want to put myself out there for judgement... like you sort of didn't know what questions to ask because you were just trying to take it in and you're trying to reflect on what you believe and things like that. For me, over time... the confidence grew and I suppose like you sort of get to the point where you're like right, I believe this and it doesn't matter whether it's different to anyone else. It's about perspectives. And you had confidence that you would not be ridiculed anyway. You know, that's my belief... and it's in a professional way that it's not going to be ripped apart or things like that, so I think it's just getting over that initial step of you're allowed to jump and wherever you fall it doesn't really matter, like we're all trying to be professional. (Education Commons: Pre-service educator)

Pre-service educators needed to be constantly encouraged to focus on their own learning and to deconstruct the ways in which participation in the learning communities impacted over time. The following excerpt illustrates the evolutionary growth that occurred as a result of regular engagement:

> I can remember sitting there having, you know, obviously once upon a time I was shy in contexts like that and I've got all my Education Commons notes at home in a folder and you have all these questions at the bottom that I was never game to ask or never got answered because I wasn't touching that microphone. But now I have, as you said, the confidence to be able to stand up and ask my questions ... I know that I can learn more by asking and likewise I enjoy responding to the questions that others ask too. We don't just leave it to the panellists anymore. Education Commons is equipping us with the things that our courses can't and using tools like the teachers and the experts in the field to give us as much knowledge and confidence so that when we do go out there we will have, oh, you know, we've got the ability to reflect critically

and we will know what to do when we don't know what to do too. (Education Commons: Pre-service educator)

A sense of self-confidence emerged, alongside a growing sense of professional identity as teacher. As one pre-service educator explained:

> Yeah, I can engage in a conversation because I know something about that. I also know now that it's not being afraid to ask questions. You're allowed to be proactive in whatever you need to be proactive in and like at the beginning you weren't game to ask questions but I think you sort of as a teacher it's important to ask questions that you don't know. (Education Commons: Pre-service educator)

From the narrative data, it is apparent that the process approach to structuring learning communities had a positive effect on the emerging professional identity of the pre-service educators. For example:

> So the panel's one thing and you grow into that obviously and in the pedagogical conversations or the conversations that we have later, we obviously try to, well our strategy is more, okay, so what's this in relation to me?...so what does it matter for me? What were the key messages that I might have got out of the conversation last time that I can talk about with others to further extend my thinking? Can you see that the conversations, that dreaded term...it's not all bad. You find yourself ... definitely in the pedagogical conversation, you hear experiences, say, from another academic or even other students now in Education Commons and immediately as teaching professionals that's the first thing we do. We're like, well, how can I adapt that to my repertoire of strategies? Or how can I apply that into my classroom? Or that's good to take note of if I'm ever placed in that situation. (Education Commons: Pre-service educator)

Participants in the learning communities were also able to deconstruct their experiences and thus challenge possibilities for well-informed and responsive practice. In traversing the terrain to 'becoming teacher', the pre-service educators felt that they had become more equipped to deal with a range of organisational structures and processes, to challenge grand narratives about the teaching profession and what it means to be a teacher and to teach, and to reframe the context to suit their needs, interests and abilities. They were learning to move within and between their multiple Discourses and identities, even though they do not always represent consistent values (Gee, 1996). For many of the pre-service educators, moving amongst Discourses had become a more seamless process, with an increased potential for a sharing of problem-solving strategies across Discourses.

DOI: 10.1057/9781137473028.0006

It also became evident as we began to interview novice teachers, who had participated in some of the projects as pre-service educators, that they carried critical reflection into their new careers. It became evident that the workings of a pedagogy of induction were providing sustainability into the future and were thus contributing to the ecological perspective of the projects.

Conclusion

Participants in the teaching–learning projects that we implemented engaged in critical reflection. This chapter demonstrated our use of the deconstruct stage of critical reflection to examine how a pedagogy of induction worked. Our deconstruction employed Gruenewald's (2003) five dimensions of place to investigate how the places and spaces of some of the projects – in particular, the FYI Program and Education Commons – were understood by participants. Specific learnings about induction and professional learning were that:

▶ participants valued the building of social relationships and the possibilities of networking with members of the teaching profession;
▶ place was important, and spaces where novices and experts could meet provided opportunities for all to learn, not just those who were novices;
▶ learning and feeling positive about teaching seemed to produce career optimism;
▶ participants appreciated being able to link previous experiences to learning about new contexts;
▶ informal learning opportunities, beyond traditional course structures, enabled participants to connect what were often discrete learning experiences;
▶ access to multiple perspectives on educational issues assisted some participants to challenge existing views and taken-for-granted 'truths' or to take a personal standpoint on particular issues;
▶ participants developed independence as well as interdependence in their learning communities;
▶ learning was often associated with the shifting of power relationships;

DOI: 10.1057/9781137473028.0006

▶ successful induction involves learning a new Discourse in a safe environment and becoming an insider;
▶ confidence develops over time and not everyone develops at the same pace;
▶ professional learning is a lifelong activity.

DOI: 10.1057/9781137473028.0006

4

Theorising a Pedagogy of Induction

Abstract: *This chapter focuses on the theorising component of a model of critical reflection as used in constructing a pedagogy of induction. It highlights the usefulness of looking beyond immediacy to explore broader theoretical and philosophical debates in relation to teacher professional learning and induction. The chapter demonstrates how, through the process of theorising, the focus becomes one of personal and professional identity building. It also provides a means of exploring relevant educational practice, big ideas and issues that are affecting the teaching profession. The theorising references important outcomes of a pedagogy of induction. These include the building of agency, the construction of professional identities through professional learning, and the enhancement of workforce capabilities and career development learning.*

Keywords: career development learning; collaborative critical reflection; futures-focus; lifelong and life-wide learning; occupational self-efficacy; pedagogy of induction

Henderson, Robyn and Karen Noble. *Professional Learning, Induction and Critical Reflection: Building Workforce Capacity in Education.* Basingstoke: Palgrave Macmillan, 2015. DOI: 10.1057/9781137473028.0007.

Introduction

This chapter focuses on the theorising component of the model of critical reflection and highlights the usefulness of looking beyond immediacy to explore broader theoretical and philosophical debates. This enables complexities within the teaching profession to be better understood. In education, the broad philosophical frames of sociology and psychology often provide the backdrop for the exploration of conscious and unconscious ways in which educators make meaning of their practice context. This chapter shows how learning can be extended beyond the literal to theorise practice from multiple perspectives. We use the question 'How might we theorise a pedagogy of induction?' to guide this chapter.

Our discussion of theorisation draws on multiple theories, just as we would expect pre-service educators to draw on multiple theories when engaging in a pedagogy of induction. Through presenting two examples of theorising, we plan to demonstrate that different theories can give different understandings about being, knowing and doing teacher and teaching. The chapter, then, is located within literatures that allow us to traverse psychological and sociological discourses. Although some would argue that an eclectic approach is not productive, our approach foregrounds the potential for multiple perspectives, a key characteristic of a pedagogy of induction. The theorising helps to reference important outcomes of the pedagogy. These include the building of agency, construction of professional identities through professional learning, enhancement of workforce capabilities and career development learning. Each of these transcends the stages of teachers' careers, as professional learning is lifelong and life-wide.

A pedagogy of induction is premised on the supposition that high attrition rates of 'new' teachers might be ameliorated if pre-service educators were encouraged and supported to build a professional identity from the outset of their studies and to begin to build professional networks. In examining data from some of the projects that inform this book, we highlight the importance of collaborative teacher talk and show how teachers can move beyond context-specific problems of practice to a consideration and synthesis of big picture educational issues. These authentic discussions can stimulate professional learning that is intrinsically motivated and self-directed and has the ability to add to teachers' knowledge and levels of awareness, regardless of the stage of their career. This focus becomes one of personal and professional identity building, with the structure of

DOI: 10.1057/9781137473028.0007

critical reflection, enabled in collaborative discussions, providing a means of exploring relevant educational practice and the issues that are affecting the profession now and might affect the profession in the future.

The use of theorising

A pedagogy of induction has been conceptualised as one that provides opportunities for participants to think deeply about aspects of educational practice, to make links between theory and practice, and to challenge existing assumptions and grand narratives in order to think about other ways of doing educational practice. Loughran (2002, 2007) regarded engagement with the identity of teacher-researcher as being key to developing a critical awareness of practice and to becoming part of the profession. This is very different from taking a technicist perspective that suggests that a teacher simply has to learn the best teaching techniques to ensure professional success.

In using the model of critical reflection (Macfarlane et al., 2006), a pedagogy of induction incorporates research. This is evident particularly in the theorise stage, where investigating how an issue might be explained, exploring what is known about the issue, and finding possible ways of working with it put pre-service educators and teachers into a researcher role. This component of teacher identity relates to coming to understand the relationships between teaching and learning in the world of work and understanding practice and its impacts on student learning. Education Commons encourages pre-service educators to traverse the field of practice and to become critically aware of significant issues and research that, when applied, support, question and challenge, or extend knowledge about existing ways of being, knowing and doing teacher and teaching. We do not want to give the impression that the only purpose of Education Commons is to challenge and critique. Rather, we see these characteristics as being essential to making sense of what it means to be a teacher. When research is included in the process, decisions about 'what to do when you don't know what to do' can then be made from a position of knowledge and understanding. A teacher's decisions should come from knowledge of available options, a rationale for why one course of action might be selected over another, and a judgement about what is likely to work in this particular context and set of circumstances at this particular time.

DOI: 10.1057/9781137473028.0007

When participants engage in collaborative critical reflection they are able to customise and individualise their learning (Henderson et al., 2013) and achieve what Ryan (2011) called 'purposeful reflection' which enables 'deep, active learning' (p. 101). It is not simply about participants making sense of their existing experiences, but rather, it extends to engaging them in the processes of reimagining future experiences. In other words, this is about shifting from understanding existing spaces and places as well as creating possibilities for new ways of understanding and operating within the places and spaces of education.

Advancing a futures-focused orientation that is indeed a transformative one – one that holds true to the tenets of a pedagogy of induction as outlined previously – requires moving beyond acceptance and maintenance of the status quo (Gur-Ze'ev et al., 2001) and encouraging participants to engage in an exploration of the complex and dynamic nature of becoming and being a teacher. Across the various projects informing the construction of a pedagogy of induction, particularly Projects 1, 2 and 3, there have been opportunities for teachers (preservice, novice and experienced) to 'engage in the complex integration of personal self' and 'a culturally scripted, often narrowly defined professional role while maintaining individuality' (Alsup, 2006, p. 4). This integration of the personal and professional self and the ways in which these can be theorised provide the focus of the remainder of this chapter.

Theorising

As outlined in previous chapters, the five projects that we have discussed are varied in their principal purposes. For example, the FYI Program focused on transition to university for Education students and what it means to become a university student. Doc Chat related predominantly to becoming an academic, while Education Commons and Education Commons International focused on induction into the world of work as teachers. In this chapter, the focus of the data and their subsequent analyses relate primarily to Education Commons and Education Commons International, as we work to demonstrate how the theorisation of a pedagogy of induction has been iterative. Our discussion emerges from the longitudinal data we have collected and collated over the duration of the projects.

DOI: 10.1057/9781137473028.0007

To achieve our aim, we have deliberately included multiple voices, including those of pre-service, novice and experienced teachers, as well as our own reflections as researchers, to illustrate how we have come to conceptualise our thinking about a pedagogy of induction. This involves thinking about how the personal and professional aspects of identity development underlie the process approach that we have instituted. However, we need to make it clear that the data and the discussion we present here provide a partial and fragmented overview of the projects. In wanting to provide some insights into the theorise stage of the model of critical reflection, we have necessarily been selective in our choice of data. In fact, the data that are presented here represent a very small selection of the overall data that were collected.

We present three sets of data. Each set consists of an excerpt from a conversation between a participant and an interviewer, along with a Wordle™ (Feinberg, 2013). The conversations were recorded during semi-structured interviews with participants from two of the projects – Education Commons and Education Commons International. Some participants had been involved in both projects. The interviews were conducted as reflective conversations, whereby the interviewer asked participants to reflect on their experiences of the relevant project/s. We have selected a section from three interviews. In many respects, however, the excerpts seem monologic. This resulted from the way that the interviews were conducted. The interviewer asked prompt questions to encourage critical reflection and where possible assumed the role of listener.

Following the presentation of each conversation, we provide a Wordle™ (Feinberg, 2013) which has been developed from the text of the conversation. This was produced by entering each of the conversations into a software program where the words were randomly configured and digitally displayed. The more times a specific word was included, the larger its font size. McNaught and Lam (2010) identified Wordle™ as a 'useful tool for preliminary analysis, and for the validation of previous findings' (p. 630). However, they also identified limitations that arise from the focus on words and the neglect of semantics, phrases and sentences. Nevertheless, we see each Wordle™ as providing some information that might illustrate the emphasis of each interviewee and might link to the conceptual tenets and praxis underpinning each conversation.

As the aim of presenting data in this chapter is to theorise a pedagogy of induction, we decided to demonstrate that each of us could come to

DOI: 10.1057/9781137473028.0007

the same set of data with different thinking and theorising. This is in keeping with the practice of critical reflection and the possibilities for multiple ways of theorising (Macfarlane et al., 2006). As we explained in earlier chapters, the approach to induction that we developed relies on the strengths that learners bring to discussions in an affinity space (Gee, 2004). In this chapter, we draw on our own strengths to demonstrate how the theorising stage of critical reflection can be utilised to unpack aspects of a pedagogy of induction. At the end of the data, we present a collective Wordle™ that was constructed from the texts of the three interviews.

To ensure that meaning is not lost across the three sets of data, we present the data first and then the analyses. We want readers to get a sense of the data in context, rather than presenting small sections of data. This allows us to theorise across the three data sets, rather than offering a piecemeal approach. We are confident that this will preserve meaning across the conversations and enable readers to see more easily resonance or otherwise between their own readings of the data and our analyses and theorisations.

The reflective conversations

Reflective conversations 1 and 2 are from panellists involved in the Education Commons topic of 'working in rural and remote contexts'. Reflective conversation 3 is from a pre-service educator who was an audience member at an Education Commons International panel event. Some details about the three reflective conversations are as follows:

▸ Reflective conversation 1 is from Jolie (pseudonym), an experienced teacher who, towards the end of her career, decided to move to an isolated community in far north Queensland, after teaching for over 30 years in rural contexts. She wanted to fulfil a desire that she had held for a long time – to work in an Indigenous community.

▸ Reflective conversation 2 is from a novice teacher who had taken a position in a rural community in south west Queensland. As a pre-service educator, Courtney (pseudonym) had attended Education Commons on a regular basis for approximately three years prior to graduation.

▸ Reflective conversation 3 is from Kaitlin (pseudonym), a fourth-year pre-service educator who participated regularly in

DOI: 10.1057/9781137473028.0007

Education Commons and was a panellist on one occasion, when she represented the student voice in a particular discussion. The context of the conversation presented here draws from her engagement as a participant/audience member in Education Commons International.

Reflective conversation 1: Jolie: experienced teacher

Jolie was an experienced teacher and she was a panellist at Education Commons when the topic was about 'working in rural and remote contexts'. As a teacher who had taught in rural schools for a long time, she was currently teaching in a remote, indigenous school.

1 J: I thought I would like to hear from others and I'm very curious about
2   promoting teachers' ongoing learning too. It's always a challenge.
3   This is what is needed especially for starting teachers – challenging
4   their perceptions of what they think the work entails, because I think
5   it is often not like what they expect. In the context of Education
6   Commons the way that everyone is sharing their experiences – that is
7   probably way more honest. For a long time I have supervised prac
8   students and I know for them there's always been a difference between
9   what's covered at uni and then suddenly you go into a practical situation
10   and there's so many other things that you also need to focus on. Often it
11   appears overwhelming as they haven't probably joined up the dots across
12   the various courses that they are doing. There is a transition into really
13   doing the job. Does that make sense? It's a curiosity, but it's more of a
14   personal rather than a professional. No it's not. I guess for me it's
15   personal, but in the same way I'm curious in a professional way for
16   knowing how to assist the newer teachers I work with in making that
17   transition, because there is a transition between really doing the job.
18   I know I've had lots of feedback over many years from students saying,
19   oh my goodness it's so different when you're actually doing this job.
20   I've taught for so long I've forgotten what it's like to, or how it would
21   maybe feel. Maybe not what it's like but how it would feel. That's why
22   I've tried to put myself in the situation that I'm in now, so that
23   you're out of your comfort zone. I sort of like that because it makes you
24   rely on other skills you might find you have or find that you need to
25   develop. Okay, I probably was very shaped by the experiences that I've
26   had in this year and I guess I am in no way daunted by the idea of rural
27   education, having been involved in that for so long. I thought it was really

DOI: 10.1057/9781137473028.0007

28 good to hear responses from people either like yourself going into that
29 situation because you're already thinking about what the challenge is that
30 you're going to come across and going to be, and yet I don't see those as
31 challenges. It was really interesting for me in terms of, I can't remember
32 the lovely year one teacher, sorry, I can't remember her name.
33 I: Courtney.
34 J: Thank you. Courtney was really good at telling what her, that she'd had
35 such a positive experience for her first year teaching and although she
36 recognised some issues that were there she could reflect on how she had
37 coped and how she had strategies for knowing what to do in challenging
38 situations. Clearly her experience has been a good one. Probably it would
39 be. We could talk to another person who maybe would not have those
40 positive experiences. Hers seemed to be a very successful year in terms of
41 what she was saying to us. I'm sure it had ups and downs and we all do
42 and we're probably inclined not to dwell on those downs. So for me that
43 was curious from the rural education side because having not lived in a
44 city for so long, I don't see that as a great challenge. It helped me see the
45 transition to a new context through her eyes – young or old, novice or
46 experienced, there are challenges to face and new ways need to be
47 adopted regardless. It's how you choose to face those challenges that
48 makes a big difference to your successful transition.

FIGURE 4.1   *Wordle 1, from Jolie's reflective conversation*

Reflective conversation 2: Courtney: novice teacher

Courtney was a beginning teacher and had completed one year of teaching. She had attended Education Commons as an undergraduate student and she continued to attend whenever she was able to attend

DOI: 10.1057/9781137473028.0007

after her graduation and transition into the teaching workforce. During her undergraduate studies, she had undertaken a voluntary Isolated Children's Project, where she was a governess on a rural property for a period of three weeks. Her experience in that project was a key determinant in her choice to apply for a rural teaching position.

1 C: It was strange to be on the other side this time as a panellist. It was hard
2   to know what to expect from that perspective. I understand now too why
3   Karen and Robyn always insisted on panellists not preparing anything in
4   advance, just coming and telling their stories and sharing their insights.
5   Anything that I thought I would say went out the window as soon as we
6   started. You kind of just bounced off what others were saying. The nerves
7   were gone quickly really and I started to get excited telling them of my
8   time in [remote town] and my experiences teaching. It was great. So while
9   I am not sure exactly what I expected and, given that I have been to so
10   many Education Commons over the years as well, it was different. As a
11   panellist I was an expert of sorts. But having been in their shoes not very
12   long ago, I also felt that I could empathise with them too. Expectations, I
13   guess more interpreting, but I felt that it was going to be an interesting
14   conversation. Because I was young and inexperienced in the field of
15   education it was a little daunting to be beside others with loads of
16   experience. So I was sitting there on the panel knowing that I was
17   interested in listening to what the other experts had to say, but also
18   reminding myself that they wanted to hear from me and about my
19   experiences too. I wasn't there just to listen! So it was like all the people
20   who were part of the Education Commons were listening to me and what I
21   had to say, which was very fulfilling, because it gave me that feeling that
22   even though I've only got 12 months under my belt and that was it, my
23   views and opinions were still very worthwhile. It was really good.
24   Particularly being able to relate to the likes of those nearly finished,
25   because they're almost graduating and I'd already done 12 months. I can
26   remember 12 months ago, basically, the position I was in and how that's
27   changed or been influenced by the year that I have had. It was almost like
28   a three-step thing. There was a fourth year student talking about her ICP
29   [Isolated Children's Program] experiences, then me, then the likes of
30   John and Jolie, both very experienced. Jolie was fabulous. Her,
31   experience is just amazing and so I enjoyed going through almost the
32   journey of teaching across all of us. Going from one to the next and being
33   able to make connections to each regardless of our levels of experience.
34 I: Did you learn something during the discussion?

DOI: 10.1057/9781137473028.0007

35 C: Of course [laughs]. What wouldn't you learn? I did learn a big thing.

36   Again, it was that how far I had come in a year compared to the position

37   you were in [fourth year student], which I remember so much, 12 months

38   ago ... All those things we talked about during the Education Commons

39   were then enacted and I've come 12 months further along. So I realised

40   that, yep, that was the first step. Then in 15 years' time, I may be in a

41   position where Jolie is, having so much experience. So I guess I learned

42   that really, it is such a continuous progression of learning, that you're

43   constantly learning new stuff. You're constantly growing as a teacher,

44   and even though you've been in it for 15, 20 years, you can still gain so

45   much day by day. I took away that I've still got a long way to go [laughs]

46   in any teaching situation. I guess that no matter which way the world is

47   going, we're constantly going to have to deal with issues, that there's no

48   way we can fix everything and then it'll all be smooth. There's constantly

49   whether, even if we fix the issues we've got now, in ten years' time, when

50   that's actually completed, we're still, there's going to be a whole new

51   bunch of issues, that we're in this constant cycle of change, that we

52   constantly need to address new issues, after new issues, after new issues.

FIGURE 4.2   *Wordle 2, from Courtney's reflective conversation*

Reflective conversation 3: Kaitlin: graduating pre-service educator

Kaitlin was a fourth-year student who participated regularly in Education Commons and Education Commons International. She was a panellist in one Education Commons event, representing the student voice in a particular discussion. In this interview, however, she draws from her

DOI: 10.1057/9781137473028.0007

engagement as an audience member at Education Commons International, with the discussion moving between panellists in Australia and the USA. Because of her experience of both projects, she was able to draw comparisons across the two and reflect on their differences and similarities.

1 K: Education Commons being international, so getting those broader views,
2   like worldly views, like how education is for them over in America
3   compared to ... Like you can sort of sit down and you could sort of see,
4   this is what we do in Australia, what do you do over there sort of thing?
5   Not just reading about it. That's powerful – it brings it to life. Obviously
6   there are things that are vastly different between the two. One of them,
7   rural and remote. Like their rural versus rural was largely different, but
8   also I had no idea – like [Name of University in the USA] being right in
9   the centre of town, great big building with no outside spaces and now I
10   think about how would their schools be different to ours sort of thing.
11   Not just physically. Like how its contexts are different to our contexts in a
12   physical environment, sort of education different. You know the thing
13   and the different sort of struggles or challenges they'd have because of the
14   different environment that they have over there compared to what we
15   have over here. What stood out for me was their understanding of critical
16   reflection and the teacher as a researcher and because I'd just done the
17   research project for our internship course that was so much more powerful
18   seeing that they sort of in America expect that sort of stuff to occur all the
19   time. That was one thing that I got from that; that it is so much more
20   effective with them for their reflection and stuff like that and how they
21   grow as professionals through research. You don't realise you're doing it.
22   Like I said, when you do the model of critical reflection and you're trying
23   to think of other ways and what theory you can draw on and think
24   otherwise and lots of stuff and theorise, you really do have to go and
25   research. Like if you don't immediately know the answer you've got to
26   somehow come up with another way or another strategy and the way
27   you're going to do that is, so research, it's really fun. You sort of see
28   that as like a main theme; like we're lifelong learners. It's hard for other
29   people outside the profession to see that, I've found. They don't see us as
30   researchers, they see it, like I've got friends who say, oh, you just finger
31   paint all day and that sort of stuff and I'm like, no, really, it's hard work.
32   It is hard work. So, yeah, just the whole research theme and to become
33   better professionals, liking to grow within the profession and stuff like
34   that. A lot of research and reflection and growth needs to occur, so ...

DOI: 10.1057/9781137473028.0007

35   Well, I sort of went away from Education Commons and I was more –
36   because I got so involved in the whole research thing with our seminar
37   presentation and then hearing what the teachers in the USA were doing in
38   their classes and stuff like that and how Tom [USA panellist in Education
39   Commons International] was doing all the gathering of data
40   and changing the children's lives using the research and helping
41   them in the classroom sort of thing and having that effect on the kids by
42   doing that. I sort of thought, you know, it's something that I would like to
43   be able to do, would be to further develop my skills to be able to not just
44   be a teacher, but I don't know, like get into all that sort of stuff and, yeah.
45   A bit like when you're teaching you talk about process and you talk about
46   content and if you've got a transformational approach to learning and
47   teaching, it's the process. It's the journey that you're taking the students
48   on that's more important than whether or not they can recall the name of
49   the first Prime Minister or whatever fact it might be. Becoming a teacher,
50   it's a personal as well as a professional journey and then we talk about the
51   importance of being connected, so whether it's personally to your family
52   and your friends and having that support network around you to help you
53   to be successful. You know, in a work context it might be, well in a
54   professional context it might be linking with other like-minded students,
55   like other education students that are equally as motivated as you and then
56   it's about connecting with your mentor teachers and starting those
57   relationships and then connecting with other teachers etcetera. Do you
58   think that we need to unpack that a little bit more for them in terms of
59   making that explicit? That what you get out of it will be different
60   depending on where you are in your journey. But it's about being in that
61   space and in that moment, just experiencing ... With uni sometimes you
62   sort of get to that point where you're like, what's it useful for? So I think
63   things like Education Commons and we've done a bit of other PD as well
64   and that's really helped us really connect back to well, it links with
65   theory, like yeah, you've got theory and then you've got your PD where
66   you get all these practicals and then you can use it in your prac and things
67   like that. So it's about building those connections ... I think everything
68   needs to work together like a big jigsaw I suppose where ... as I said
69   before, that confidence, that readiness to just be out in a classroom and
70   that I am a teacher now, I'm ready. I don't think I would never have got
71   there, but I do think that it's helped me get there faster. Like, if I hadn't
72   have gone to Education Commons I would still be back a little bit. I'd still
73   be behind if that makes sense? But I think it has helped me in terms of my

74 own confidence, it's come much earlier ... I also have a positive
75 perception of my ability. I see myself as a teacher. You think really
76 deeply about how you're going to phrase a question for example, because
77 you now know that you can match it with teachers and others in that
78 context. It's been interesting because even though you're a teacher
79 and you're supposed to be influencing children in a good way to be active
80 citizens, it is clear that you're still able to have your own
81 individual sort of journey, your way. I think having seen all the teachers
82 and experts come in and have different perspectives sort of opened that up
83 for me, that I'm not going to follow in everyone else's footsteps ... You
84 don't have to emulate someone else ... you've learned how you can
85 express your opinion but also how you can receive somebody else's
86 opinion that might be different to yours and critically reflect on it and
87 come to a position of yeah, okay, well that challenges my thinking and
88 therefore my thinking might change as a consequence of it, or well no,
89 that's just further entrenched my perspective ... Well like a sponge, you
90 can take it all in and you don't know when you're getting to saturation
91 point but you just sit there and let the water keep running over just in case
92 there's anything more you can soak up. Whereas prac, it's a bit more
93 threatening because you are getting assessed and you need to start
94 knowing things. Education Commons is more relaxed, non-threatening
95 and no expectations.

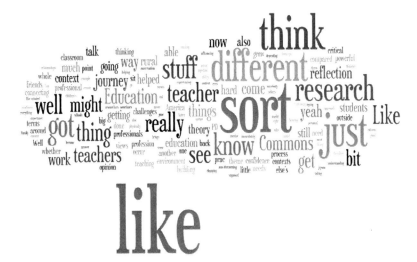

FIGURE 4.3   *Wordle 3, from Kaitlin's reflective conversation*

DOI: 10.1057/9781137473028.0007

FIGURE 4.4   *Wordle 4, a collective illustration from the reflective conversations of Jolie, Courtney and Kaitlin*

Theorising: Robyn's discussion

In thinking about the data, I use a lens that frames the social, cultural and discursive practices of interactions and of teaching. I theorise education as a social and cultural practice. This includes the teaching of pre-service educators in the university context, as well as the education of students in schools and the ongoing professional learning of teachers. All of these contexts were discussed during the reflective conversations from Jolie, Courtney and Kaitlin.

By understanding education as a social and cultural practice, we have to consider its location within social, cultural, moral and political relationships. If we apply the theorisation described by Chouliaraki and Fairclough (1999), we understand that social practices are shaped, constrained and maintained by the 'relative permanencies' of social structures (p. 22). At the same time, however, they are practices of production and 'particular people in particular relationships using particular resources' can transform social structures (p. 23). This view of the social world recognises that social life can be constrained by social structures and that there is also the potential for change through the effects of agency and the possibilities for creativity and social transformation. This thinking is useful for considering the data we collected, because it allows for social practices to be understood as points of connection between social structures and individual actions. This relationship is dialectical, operating in both directions and constraining and enabling at the same time (Chouliaraki & Fairclough, 1999; Harvey, 1996; Henderson, Abawi,

DOI: 10.1057/9781137473028.0007

& Conway, 2011). Even though this thinking has drawn criticism because of its circularity (Harvey, 1996), it is helpful for making sense of educational practice as being contextually situated, dynamic, and open to change (Henderson et al., 2011).

I also consider the relationship between text – the reflective conversations and Wordle™ illustrations – and context (Fairclough, 2001). The three reflective conversations, produced by Jolie, Courtney and Kaitlin, are embedded in several layers of context. They are located within the interviews where they were constructed, but they also sit within Jolie's and Courtney's participation in a particular Education Commons panel discussion and Kaitlin's participation as an audience member in an Education Commons International discussion. Additionally, the reflective conversations are located in the broader contexts of schools and universities, education systems, society more generally, and the discursive practices and ways of working that are encourage and valued (Henderson et al., 2011) within these contexts.

The reflective conversations were constructed by the three teachers and demonstrate their differing levels of experience: Jolie, as an experienced teacher with over 30 years in schools; Courtney as a novice teacher with one year's experience; and Kaitlin as a graduating pre-service educator/ teacher. Their conversations provide clues to their work contexts and their levels of experience. It seemed that Jolie's extensive experience as a teacher enabled her to talk about issues that she regarded as of concern to those with leadership roles in schools: 'promoting teachers' ongoing learning' (Jolie, line 2) and challenging new teachers' assumptions (Jolie, lines 3–4). She also mentioned her experiences of mentoring pre-service and beginning teachers and the 'difference between what's covered at uni' and the 'practical situation' (Jolie, lines 8–9). The Wordle™ of Jodie's conversation, shown in Figure 4.1, demonstrates her concern with transition. Although the Wordle™ simply provides information about the frequency of word use, the transitions experienced by teachers were an important focus in Jolie's reflective conversation.

In contrast to Jolie's concern with assisting the transition and induction of new teachers into the world of work, Courtney talked about her own transition from learner in the university context to novice teacher in a school. Her understanding about this was evident when she talked about her participation in Education Commons. She explained that she 'wasn't there just to listen!' (Courtney, line 19) because she was expected to be 'an expert of sorts' (Courtney, line 11). She indicated that she could empathise with pre-service educators as she had 'been in their shoes not very long

DOI: 10.1057/9781137473028.0007

ago' (Courtney, lines 11–12). Courtney's Wordle™ in Figure 4.2 indicates her concern with time and with her experiences developing over time. Frequently used words included *time, year, years, months* and *constantly*.

Kaitlin, who was a pre-service teacher about to graduate, was future-focused in the types of topics that she discussed. She identified several things that 'might be' or that she 'would like to be able to do' in her future teaching (Kaitlin, lines 42, 54). The Wordle™ representation of Kaitlin's reflective conversation, shown in Figure 4.3, also seems to indicate her considerations of the future. Many of the frequently used words were those from her everyday language (for example, *sort, like, really*), combined with her views about *Education, teaching,* and the *journey* she was undertaking.

Despite the teachers' differing levels of experience, their reflective conversations suggested the importance of ongoing professional learning and being a lifelong learner: 'you're constantly learning new stuff' (Courtney, lines 42–43), 'you're constantly growing as a teacher' (Courtney, line 43), 'we're lifelong learners' (Kaitlin, line 28). Jolie as the experienced teacher, however, suggested that those who have 'taught for so long' sometimes forget 'what it's like' and 'how it would feel' to not have particular skills (Jolie, lines 20–21). She indicated that stepping 'out of your comfort zone' (Jolie, line 23) will help to develop new skills, even for experienced teachers like herself.

For all three teachers, participation in the processes of a pedagogy of induction (through Education Commons and Education Commons International) had benefits. These included learning from others' experiences (Jolie, line 6; Courtney, lines 28–33; Kaitlin, lines 1–2), making connections (Courtney, line 33; Kaitlin, lines 3–5), reflecting on experience (Jolie, lines 25–26; Courtney, line 36; Kaitlin, lines 71–73), and thinking about future challenges (Jolie, lines 29–30; Courtney, lines 40–43; Kaitlin, lines 42–44).

It was apparent in the reflective conversations that all three teachers considered themselves to be agentic. Their talk implied a sense of enablement and an ability to tackle new challenges (Jolie, lines 22–23; Courtney, line 52; Kaitlin, line 28) and to develop both personally and professionally (Jolie, lines 13–17; Courtney, line 43; Kaitlin, line 50). There was no dwelling on the constraints that schooling can present. This silence in the data suggested that all three teachers were comfortable with their teacher and professional identities. As Kaitlin explained: 'I also have a positive perception of my ability. I see myself as a teacher' (Kaitlin, lines 74–75). It appeared that Jolie, Courtney and Kaitlin had been enabled by their experiences and their thinking about teaching and learning.

DOI: 10.1057/9781137473028.0007

Theorising: Karen's discussion

In keeping with the practice of critical reflection and the possibilities for multiple ways of theorising, my analysis is through the lens of social constructivism and the career development learning approach of the systems theory framework (McMahon & Patton, 1995; Patton & McMahon, 1999, 2006). A career development learning perspective enables a reading of the discursive and inter-related contexts against which each of the three teachers' experiences of professional learning has influenced, or may influence, their professional identity.

In light of the complexity of professional identity development (Davey, 2013), metacognitive awareness of how to mobilise discourses that will create, affirm and sustain oneself throughout experiences in the workplace is critical. That is, to understand ways of being, knowing and doing teacher professional learning, as a process of professional identity formation, can empower teachers to resist discourses of power and control and to privilege reflexivity, critical consciousness, learning, transformation and action for social construction (Noble & McIlveen, 2012). This imagines new ways of understanding oneself as teacher and developing a career in teaching. Understanding how the self develops in context is critical to individual self-actualisation as a professional, as well as being essential for the development and renewal of the profession more broadly. These ideas draw on the premise that the individual and the profession are discursively produced and socially constructed.

The systems theory framework (McMahon & Patton, 1995; Patton & McMahon, 1999, 2006) of careers integrates traditional with emerging theories. It fits well with our multiple perspectives approach, by providing a broad, contextualised view of career and allowing for an exploration of overlapping systems of influence, including individual, social and environmental systems (McIlveen & Patton, 2007). These are dynamically relational in nature and characterised in terms of recursiveness, change over time, and chance.

In understanding the motivations for engagement in professional learning and the plethora of systems that interact to influence career aspirations and development and personal and professional efficacy, chance, hope and optimism are highlighted. They are inherent in the process of attending to problems of practice and demonstrate the connectivity between the world of work and the impact of practice on ongoing professional learning. That is, occupational self-efficacy is affected by multiple contexts and experiences and the interactions that take place as a consequence of engagement

DOI: 10.1057/9781137473028.0007

across these, not simply personal or individual personality dispositions. Furthermore, taking a life-wide and lifelong approach to professional learning through a pedagogy of induction into a profession can shift the focus from an individual lens to a collective one, thus exploring the potential for workforce capacity building within the teaching profession. Therefore, the connection of psychological and sociological ways of understanding learning and the world of work become useful.

Just as Robyn's analysis discussed the constraining effect that social structures sometimes have, my analysis focuses on the macro and the micro systems and structures that influence professional learning. However, my specific focus is on the aspects of engagement in professional learning opportunities that participants identified as impacting their career optimism or their satisfaction with career. I am particularly interested in elaborating how they describe behavioural changes as a consequence of their engagement in this model of professional learning, and how over time this learning may in fact influence career optimism.

As a point of departure from Robyn's approach, I present my thematic analysis in a table format, followed by a descriptive discussion. These connect the visual and textual data. References made by Jolie, Courtney and Kaitlin to the three constructs of career development are shown in Table 4.1. Although I have altered the exact language, I have maintained the intent or meaning conveyed within the reflective conversations.

I draw from these analyses understandings about how the contexts of professional learning interact with three key, inter-related domains of career development: conscientiousness (in terms of personal dispositions), self-efficacy and optimism (in terms of motivational dispositions) (see Carver & Scheier, 2014; McIlveen, Burton, & Beccaria, 2013; Rottinghaus, Day, & Borgen, 2005). I highlight the ways in which the participants conceptualise career optimism, understood as holding a positive disposition and positive expectations for future career outcomes (Carver & Scheier, 2014). I used the four Wordle™ illustrations (Figures 4.1–4.4) for preliminary analysis (McNaught & Lam, 2010), exploring the main differences and possible points of interest. This provided a direction for the more detailed thematic analysis of the reflective conversations.

Making sense of the data through the lens of the systems theory framework requires an understanding of career development as dynamic, fluid, recursive and subject to change over time, as well as impacted by chance (Patton & McMahon, 1999). All systems are open to influence and are inextricably linked and located within the context of time, place and space. This moves the notion of career away from the traditional linear approach that has historically shaped psychological descriptions of career counselling or vocational psychology.

TABLE 4.1   *Jolie, Courtney and Kaitlin's references to constructs of career development*

Constructs	Jolie (Figure 4.1)	Courtney (Figure 4.2)	Kaitlin (Figure 4.3)	Collective
Conscientiousness	Self-reflection	Constantly prioritise needs	Confidence	Experiential learning
	Knowing students Supporting learning	Learn from experiences Constantly challenged Listening Knowing Reflecting Able	Reflection Challenges	Reflection on and supporting learning Active engagement in learning
Self-efficacy	Successful experiences Positive interactions with others	Learning new ways Experiences	Understanding contexts Accepting difference and diversity	World of work Knowledge – experiences Contextual understandings
	Knowing context Adaptable		Experience moving from novice to expert	
Career optimism	Curious	Time	Journey	Ongoing learning journey
	New knowledge and experiences Continually learning	Continuous learning journey Support	Research	

The words in Figures 4.1–4.4 foreground the dynamic nature of professional learning with references to constantly prioritising, challenging, questioning, reflecting, continuous learning and journey. These illustrate that 'being a teacher' and 'doing teaching' are always changing and are dependent on other influences, such as social, organisational and environmental dimensions of place and space. Evidence of the fluidity of professional learning is also apparent across the three reflective conversations.

DOI: 10.1057/9781137473028.0007

For example, in Reflective Conversation 1, Jolie refers to teaching as always being a challenge, regardless of years of experience. She explains that it is often the difference between perceptions and the actual reality and totality of the work that is daunting to beginning teachers (Jolie, lines 2–7, 18–19). She also makes reference to the commentary of another panellist who was a novice teacher with limited experience in a rural context (Jolie, lines 34–38). Jolie highlighted that effective ongoing professional learning is relational in nature. For example, she referred to the challenges of making the 'transition to a new context' and the way that all teachers, whether 'young or old, novice or experienced' experience challenges (Jolie, lines 45–48).

This excerpt also speaks to conscientiousness, identified as one of the big five personality traits within the psychological literature (Costa & McCrae, 1992), and positively correlates to notions of persistence and resilience as impacting successful transition into and across the teaching profession. In contrast, Kaitlin, in Reflective Conversation 3, foregrounds independence and interdependence as contributing to conscientiousness and to building professional self-efficacy and self-confidence as she makes the transition to the field (see Kaitlin, lines 81–89).

Looking across the three reflective conversations, all three referenced the importance of professional learning in building career agency and made connections between personal and professional identity development through participation in Education Commons and/or Education Commons International. Jolie (lines 13–17) connected professional learning to a sense of curiosity and described such learning as being simultaneously personal and professional. She also made reference to gaining better understandings of diverse ways of understanding the experience of professional transition as being helpful in her support of other colleagues in her practice context. Courtney (lines 10–23) highlighted her understandings of self as being situated and understood that her own experiences could contribute to others' learning. Kaitlin (lines 2–15) emphasised the comparing and contrasting of experiences across contexts as pivotal to the positive impact that Education Commons International had on her professional learning. Her exploration of the construction of teacher as researcher helped to draw analogies between the model of critical reflection and the processes of research-led teaching and learning (Kaitlin, lines 19–28).

Each of the participants seemed to recognise our attempts to give a renewed emphasis to the importance of a positive approach to professional learning and this seems to link to positive psychology and particularly to the emerging field of positive organisational behaviour (Luthans,

DOI: 10.1057/9781137473028.0007

2002; Luthans & Youssef, 2007), That is, there seemed to be recognition of the privileging of a strengths-based approach as contributing positively to the profession and that, regardless of career stage, all participants are able to strengthen the interactions and learning experiences for all.

Conclusion

We recognise that our analyses are considerably more detailed than would ever be possible in a panel discussion at Education Commons or Education Commons International. However, our purpose in this chapter was to demonstrate how the theorise stage of the model of critical reflection (Macfarlane et al., 2006) could be applied to unpack a pedagogy of induction. Rather than understanding the theorise stage as finding the 'right' way of teasing out underpinning theory, we accept that multiple perspectives and multiple theories are possible. Indeed, the application of different theoretical lenses helps to broaden understandings. For example, in our analyses, we demonstrated that both sociological and psychological theories could be applied. Overall, our findings indicated that a pedagogy of induction helps to:

▸ move beyond the immediate context to explore broader theoretical and philosophical debates in the field of education;
▸ enhance professional learning and career development;
▸ engage in collaborative sharing of experience and collaborative problem-solving;
▸ build personal identity as well as professional identity;
▸ build agency.

These outcomes of a pedagogy of induction are likely, then, to enhance workforce capacity in education. If the outcomes enable teachers to 'know what to do when they don't know what to do', then they are well prepared to deal with any challenges that teaching might present. There is a plethora of evidence that participation in well-designed and well-funded programs significantly improve novice teachers' perceptions of themselves as professionals exhibiting a high degree of professionalism (Brock & Grady, 1998; Darling-Hammond, 2003; Loughran, 2006, 2010; Noble, Henderson, & Cross, 2013).

DOI: 10.1057/9781137473028.0007

5
Thinking Otherwise about Professional Induction

Abstract: *This chapter examines the impact of engagement in a pedagogy of induction on the transition of novice teachers to the world of work. It advocates for ongoing research on the effects of induction programs and professional learning on new teachers' experiences and their sense of efficacy, as these may provide ways of redressing high attrition from the profession in the beginning stages of a career. Poststructural theories offer a foundation for challenging taken-for-granted understandings about education and create spaces for imagining alternative ways of being, knowing and doing teaching. The voices of novice teachers are represented in the research data and emphasise the effectiveness of collaborative critical reflection as a sustaining force in initial induction and transition.*

Keywords: agency; critical reflection; efficacy; pedagogy of induction; professional induction; transition

Henderson, Robyn and Karen Noble. *Professional Learning, Induction and Critical Reflection: Building Workforce Capacity in Education.* Basingstoke: Palgrave Macmillan, 2015. DOI: 10.1057/9781137473028.0008.

DOI: 10.1057/9781137473028.0008

Introduction

Professional induction involves identification of the challenges that teachers may face and the provision of support to assist them in dealing with those challenges. A change in context can require induction processes to support transition across the stages of a career. As stated in earlier chapters, the predominant research focus of Projects 1, 2 and 3 was in relation to induction and professional learning in initial teacher education. We pointed out that Project 3 (the FYI Program) was developed to support the transition into Education study at university, while Projects 1 and 2 focused on preparing for the transition from university to the teaching workforce.

Within the research literature, the predominant focus on the development of teacher professionalism is squarely focused within the practice context, with the pre-service period of learning and development most often dealt with as a separate issue. Our focus in this book, however, has been on professional induction for future teachers from the beginning of Education study and we hope that our research goes some way towards redressing the imbalance in the literature.

To this point in the book, we have emphasised the initial stages of induction to the teaching profession – one of self-identifying as a member of the profession and becoming comfortable in the places and spaces of teacher and teaching. We also think that it is fruitful to look at how participation in these types of professional induction programs might have affected those who have made the transition from university to the world of educational work. In this chapter, then, we move beyond researching and evaluating the initial projects that informed our theorising of a pedagogy of induction, to synthesise our theory and future practice – to challenge ourselves as researchers and teacher educators to 'think otherwise' about our own practices.

Transition to the world of work

We recognise the plethora of literature that supports systemic induction programs for novices as they transition to the workplace through good mentoring (Darling-Hammond, 2003; Loughran, 2006, 2010; Murray, 2012, 2014). However, we are cognisant of the fact that even with such initiatives it is possible that 'practice shock' (Buchberger, Campos, Kallos,

DOI: 10.1057/9781137473028.0008

& Stephenson, 2001) may still occur. Thus, attention to this potential blind spot is warranted. In thinking about this, we have extended our focus to a career-wide view of transition and change, in terms of professional induction and the potential for agency, both professional and personal. After all, as we have highlighted in Chapter 3 using Gruenewald's (2003) notion of spatial imaginaries and in Chapter 4 by way of Patton and McMahon's (McMahon & Patton, 1995; Patton & McMahon, 2006) construction of a systems theory framework, understandings about place and space are fluid and dynamic. In fact, there are a multitude of influences on personal and professional identity at any point in time (Davey, 2013).

There is also a wealth of research that suggests that novice teachers who are confident and competent can have a great impact on student learning outcomes (Darling-Hammond, 2000; Wilson, Floden, & Ferrini-Mundy, 2001). The literature suggests that until novice teachers have survived the initial 'shock' of their transition into the workforce, they are unable to focus on the complexities of planning their future career trajectories or to concentrate fully on individualising their pedagogy to cater for individual student needs and to enhance learning outcomes (Keogh, Garvis, Pendergast, & Diamond, 2012; Marshall, Fittinghoff, & Cheney, 1990). Indeed, some argue that without adequate mentoring and supports, many will not survive the initial transition to the world of work (Colbert & Wolfe, 1992; Noble, 2009; Van Rensburg, Noble, & McIlveen, in press).

It often seems to be the case that beginning teachers are placed in hard-to-staff locations and, in the Australian context, that often means rural and remote localities which can present their own challenges and complexities. The experiences – or influences, as Patton and McMahon's (2006) systems theory framework would suggest – that are encountered by beginning teachers in their transition to the workplace can contribute to dissatisfaction, isolation, burnout and an increased intention to leave the profession (Fantilli & McDougall, 2009). In addressing these issues, we wanted to explore whether a pedagogy of induction from the outset of pre-service teacher education contributes to retention of teachers in the workplace.

Novice teachers' voices

Much of the literature pertaining to teacher induction and mentorship is void of the novice teacher voice. In this chapter, we attempt to rebalance

DOI: 10.1057/9781137473028.0008

the status quo somewhat, presenting narratives from three novice teachers who have experienced a pedagogy of induction from the commencement of their pre-service degree programs and who have successfully made the transition to various practice contexts. This means that we are taking a longitudinal perspective to professional induction.

The teachers' reflections on their transition from University to their school contexts highlight the opportunities and challenges that they have experienced. In particular, they provide their perceptions of the impact of context on this transition period, while at the same time reviewing the impact of the model of critical reflection on their perceived professional identity. Each of the participants whose data feature in this chapter has been in the workplace for a period greater than two years. Therefore, a degree of distance exists between their experiences at university and their experiences in the workplace. Their reflections are theorised from multiple perspectives and, in particular, a strong focus on poststructuralist theories permeates the analysis.

Theorising to 'think otherwise'

Poststructural theories offer a foundation for challenging taken-for-granted notions of performativity and instead create spaces for the imagining of alternative ways of being, knowing and doing teacher and teaching. Data collected from participants across all five projects have indicated the importance of understandings about professional learning (Loughran, 2010) and agency to challenge grand narratives about what it means to be a teacher and to teach. This provides potential for conceptual and figurative connections about teacher and teaching to be re-imagined.

The data for this chapter are drawn from reflective narratives from three novice teachers who participated in Education Commons and Education Commons International from the outset of their teacher education and who have now been in the field of practice for two years or longer. Our intention in this undertaking is not merely to discuss the reality faced by these novice teachers, but rather we aim to think more deeply about their experiences. Incorporating their voices allows us, as researchers, to derive insight and understanding to inform our current and future work in this area. Specifically, the intent here is to illustrate how the process of collaborative critical reflection has influenced or impacted the teachers'

DOI: 10.1057/9781137473028.0008

transition to the world of work. In doing this, we explore induction and professional learning as an individual and collaborative process, rather than privileging a content focus that is often narrowed to assurance of organisational priorities.

Using the data to inform our thinking

Following our longitudinal research design, the three teachers' voices featured in this chapter are the result of ongoing contact with Education Commons participants who have made the transition to the world of teaching. All three of these novice teachers were placed in 'hard to staff' areas of rural and remote Queensland and they have remained in their initial school placements for two years or more. Each of the teachers was asked to provide a written response to a series of open-ended questions pertaining to the impact that the model of critical reflection has had on their practice. As with some of the other data examples in this book, we want to give a sense of the data before we offer any form of analysis. To do this, we begin with the questions that were asked, accompanied by the data in verbatim form to foreground the novice teachers' voices. From their responses, we have drawn key themes that illustrate how the novice teacher voice informs our conceptualisation of the framework for a pedagogy of induction.

Question 1: what (if any) impact has the model of critical reflection had on your classroom practice?

Daisy

The model of critical reflection was primary in my reflection in my first year of teaching especially. I found it very difficult settling in to a new school, which was very structured and had such high expectations for its staff. I felt I was never good enough and constantly had to reflect on what I was doing to be good enough for what was expected of me. Due to feeling so pressured and stressed to exceed the expectations of our school leaders I always felt that Uni practical experiences and some tutorials, lectures, etcetera, didn't set me up for what I was in for. I therefore feel that the model of critical reflection has been the one thing that I was taught at University that was actually useful in my teaching. I was lucky enough to be able to have a mentor for

DOI: 10.1057/9781137473028.0008

the first six months of my teaching after I had said to my principal how stressed and unprepared for teaching I was. My mentor was the deputy who was a straight talker and no bull kind of person. He wouldn't sugar-coat his feedback and at times I felt like crying, but it was *exactly* what I needed. If it wasn't for my mentor I wouldn't be as reflective as I am now because he encouraged me to engage with the model of critical reflection in a positive way.

Currently our school's administration team also has a high level of expectation that as part of our coaching and mentoring program that we continually reflect on our practice. Often administration staff expect you to reflect on your teaching but don't give you the tools to do it. I'm lucky enough that I had this embedded in my learning whilst at Uni so that it is a tool that I can use to review my teaching practices.

Over the last two years of my teaching our school has changed a lot due to our admin team reflecting on regional demands and needs of our students and the expectation of high quality teaching is continually being pushed. As part of our curriculum intent and quality teaching, we complete five-week data cycles and reflection is key to this at the end of the cycle. Our students complete pre-assessment tasks, complete the learning for the unit and are summatively assessed or monitored every five weeks in line with the Australian Curriculum five week units. In line with this our students create for themselves goals for each unit for English, Mathematics and Reading. So we have to teach our students a way to reflect and review their learning and what they need to do to continually reach their goals, so I have evidently been passing down to my students how to reflect on their work as well. As much as it's important for our students to reach their goals, it is the teacher's responsibility to reflect on the distance travelled from pre-assessment to post-assessment for each student. The model of critical reflection has enabled me to do this and constantly improve my teaching and feel confident to try new strategies or see things in a different perspective.

Kitt

The model of critical reflection has had and continues to have a significant impact on both my teaching and my classroom. The model of critical reflection has given me a time and method to reflect with purpose on the many developing and continuing issues that arise.

DOI: 10.1057/9781137473028.0008

It has given me the chance to find appropriate solutions to many classroom management issues. It has given me the chance to reflect on my teaching, giving me clear and focused improvements and areas in which to grow. I have used the model of critical reflection on both a positive note and a negative. It is fantastic to use as a reflection method on not just the negative issues that arise within the classroom and teaching, but within the positive experiences as well. I find the model of critical reflection on positive experiences allows my confidence and self-esteem to grow and gives me that gentle reminder that 'I love this job' and I actually know what I am doing.

Poppy

Teaching Kindy (eKindy) through distance education instead of a traditional classroom requires me to think and reflect and think otherwise quite often, as I need to think how I can adapt ideas to make them web-based. I also try to keep activities as hands on as possible so working in the digital space is a challenge in terms of translating from a face-to-face way of working to an online one. I find that after each lesson that I always think about how the lesson went, what went well? What didn't go well? What would I do again? And what would I change?

Question 2: how is the model of critical reflection (deconstruct, confront, theorise, think otherwise) reflected in your approach to ongoing professional learning?

Daisy

Our schools culture of reflective practice has meant that having to reflect constantly enables you to identify strengths and weaknesses to see where professional learning needs to occur. Whether it's researching new activities for guided reading or having a discussion with a senior teacher in the school on how to 'chunk' units to get through our ridiculous amounts of curriculum content, it seems that the model of critical reflection makes you more realistic in your needs to better yourself than trying to back yourself and say, 'Yes I do that well. I don't need to change anything'.

It has made me realise that even if something is working well it doesn't mean you can't try something different. My first year of teaching seemed to be about getting a handle on the big stuff,

DOI: 10.1057/9781137473028.0008

behaviour management, planning and teaching. My second year gave me the ability to use the model of critical reflection in more refined areas such as 'Why aren't my kids moving reading levels? I'm doing what I did last year in guided reading and it worked then'. It meant that I had to see where my students needed to travel and getting them there needed to change. I used the model of critical reflection and realised that my students were not being exposed to various texts types regularly enough, as the English units were mainly based around narratives. It meant that during units teaching narratives I had to support their reading by including different texts types in my guided reading and writing task activities in reading groups. It meant that I had to research and find listening posts that were based around factual texts that at the end included comprehension questions such as the Literacy Network books. It meant that I could try something different and then reflect on it again to see how it really went and what needs to be refined further.

Kitt

Teaching as everyone knows is a lifelong journey. It is forever changing. The model of critical reflection helps me target the areas that I need to change or learn more in. Through the use of the model I am able to target where my professional learning needs to be. On the other side, after professional learning, a model of critical reflection is required to ensure that what knowledge and skills have been gained are appropriate to you as a teacher and to the children in your classroom. Is this what is best for them? Is this appropriate practice? What else supports this? Are there alternatives?

Poppy

I believe as a teacher you are always learning. I think when you reflect you are able to see whether a process or idea is working or not. Theorising and thinking otherwise help me to think about my context and how to make something more user-effective. For example, last year I had trouble getting families to send me feedback on their child's learning so I have developed a new way for families to send me feedback. When doing this I had to think about it being user-friendly for parents (easy to use and understand, keeping in mind that they are parents not trained teachers), very clear expectations, and making sure it won't take parents too long to do (as the parents are often time

DOI: 10.1057/9781137473028.0008

poor). During the term/semester I will reflect on how my new system is working and encourage families to give me feedback as well.

Question 3: do you still engage with the model of critical reflection? If yes, how? Is it done alone or in collaboration with others? If no, why not?

Daisy

I still engage with the model of critical reflection regularly. After leaving Uni it was something that was in-built and I did all the time. It also helped having the context that I was teaching in, as I was forced to reflect on my practice to keep my boss happy and my students moving in their development. Student results don't improve unless you reflect and refine your teaching practice. Students don't see that they need to improve their results unless they reflect on their learning needs, strengths and challenges.

Every term as part of our 'data talks' with the principal we have to reflect on our teaching and student results. If it wasn't for the model of critical reflection I would not have a framework to follow, to realistically reflect on my practice in partnership with my principal. It's easy for a teacher to point the finger at the student and say, 'Oh it wasn't their interest area', or, 'The students never listen in class. That's why they never progress'. It's much harder for a teacher to turn around and admit they could have done things differently and that their practice needs to change. Reflection of this kind needs a framework. I am paid to teach and I am paid to do it as effectively as possible so I feel it is my duty to my 'paying customers' that I give them my best self, so I feel it's a necessity to reflect using a framework.

Explicit teaching requires a teacher to be reflective. Explicit teaching, in my experience, is what moves students towards their goals. Therefore, a framework to guide the reflection is necessary. Having this kind of thing in-built into pre-service teachers before they leave Uni is what's necessary to support them and keep them in the profession longer, making them more resilient to the challenges of teaching.

Kitt

Absolutely. The model of critical reflection becomes so unconscious, that at times you don't realise you have completed it until after.

DOI: 10.1057/9781137473028.0008

I use the model of critical reflection both in collaboration and independently. I feel that sometimes the model of critical reflection warrants two heads instead of one. Other times it is more effective on your own. The model of critical reflection allows a school/team to come together as a collective to tackle large issues from a school level and has provided me and my school with success.

Poppy

Not in a formal way but I always reflect during and after lessons and activity days. If I have done an activity day (face-to-face day with the children), if it was with somebody else we will reflect on the day together usually during the trip back to [western Queensland town]. I reflect on:

▸ what worked well;
▸ what problems arise;
▸ how can I stop these problems happening again in the future?
▸ what I can do to extend children's learning?

Question 4: what effect does the context of your teaching have on your ongoing professional learning? Can you describe this?

Daisy

My context has forced me to continually reflect and seek learning opportunities to better myself. I have recently engaged in a 'Watching Others Work' program, where I reflected on my spelling pedagogy and I found it was just not getting my students pleasing results and they were not retaining the learning. I then asked my principal if I could watch another teacher teach spelling lessons and see what needed to change. I engaged in the lesson and used the model of critical reflection framework in discussions with the other teacher about the spelling lessons.

This kind of practice and the reflective people in our context meant that as a whole school we ended up reflecting on our spelling program and saw that our staff required resources and support. Due to this, we have now implemented the [name of program] and are engaging in sharing resources, ideas and working collegially as a team to better our students' spelling retention. This also saw our students' reading

DOI: 10.1057/9781137473028.0008

improve as their decoding was improving and it also supported our students who were reluctant to undertake writing tasks as they thought they were not good at spelling. I was also able to speak with my students and talk to them openly about what was working, why some things weren't working, coming up with ways to fix the problem and where can we go for help. It's a culture of teaching our students to be ongoing learners and not to just give up but reflect and see how we can realistically improve.

Kitt

My current context is a very challenging one. The biggest impact is distance. I am considerably isolated from professional learning. It is only within my own school and staff members that we are able to create professional conversations and learning. I have had a hard three years dealing with significantly high special needs with limited understanding and limited professional learning. The model of critical reflection has assisted me in really targeting what it is I need to know, learn and do, to ensure my students achieve under these circumstances.

Poppy

I think my context has a lot to do with my professional learning. Being in a remote area, there are less kindy-relevant professional development areas. Being a teacher through distance education, I am supporting parents in teaching their children, so I am providing them with ideas on what to teach and how they can teach their children. When I started teaching eKindy, I required a lot of professional development to assist me in teaching kindy through distance education as I had never had experience in this context. It was extremely beneficial to be shown how to use web-conferencing and being able to observe other teachers so that I could get my head around what I needed to do.

This year I will be working in collaboration with a small school to deliver the eKindy program. As this is new to me I will be collaborating with other eKindy teachers (who have facilitated eKindy in a small school previously) in professional learning to help facilitate this. I will also be doing plenty of reflecting on what I do and how I do it so I can do my job as efficiently as possible.

DOI: 10.1057/9781137473028.0008

Question 5: what impact does your ongoing professional learning have on student learning? How do you try to measure that?

Daisy

The impact of ongoing professional learning on student learning means that you create resilient and reflective learners, because as a teacher you are always learning new ways and implementing new strategies to support your students through reflection. It meant that my students have more opportunities to help themselves and others. This year (my second year) saw me reflect on the way I allowed students to interact in the classroom. In my first year I was so driven to have my students to work independently 90 per cent of the time they were in the classroom, they weren't allowed to sit in groups and talk during class.

This was until I had a new teaching partner, who is very experienced. She made me reflect on the way my students interacted in the classroom and see that my students were capable of teaching their peers and retaining more of the content taught in class by teaching another. We called this peer tutoring in our classes and our students were keen to support each other, listen to advice and improve their work. Any opportunity the students had to learn from one another the happier they were. They were excited to get stuck into some juicy unit work, particularly writing which, for most of my students last year, was a challenge. Of course, this strategy is written in many professional journal articles, but until I saw I needed to change I wasn't implementing these 'best practices'.

Kitt

The professional learning that takes places in my context directly impacts on my students, their learning and wellbeing. Through independent and school level critical reflection, I am able to directly target my professional learning as best as I can so that students are getting exactly what they need from me. I measure the need and success of this through using the model of critical reflection.

Poppy

As I said earlier as a teacher I believe I am always learning and when I do professional development it is usually on something to improve my

DOI: 10.1057/9781137473028.0008

teaching. The more knowledge and understanding I have on a topic the more equipped I am to efficiently teach my students. When I teach something, I check children's understanding by using questioning, observing their engagement and documenting their learning. I also think having other teachers/principals etcetera observing my teaching and giving me constructive feedback is also really helpful and goes a long way to improve my teaching practices. I can use the model of critical reflection to ensure that we are all focusing on the same things. I learned that from prac at Uni – it helps keep things professionally focused and helps me to avoid personalising others' comments too.

Themes from the teachers' responses about impact

The themes that we have drawn from the three teachers' responses include:

▶ the model of critical reflection as a survival tool for initial transition to the world of work;
▶ knowing and using the reflective tool of the model of critical reflection can improve practice and build understandings about being a professional;
▶ using the model of critical reflection supports collective action.

In the next sections, we expand on each of these key themes and reflect on how this knowledge has impacted on our thinking about a pedagogy of induction.

Critical reflection as a survival tool for initial transition to work

Professional educators often advocate reflective practice. Indeed, there is an expectation in the Australian *National professional standards for teachers* (Australian Institute for Teaching and School Leadership, 2011) that they engage in professional learning (Standard 6) by seeking and applying constructive feedback to improve practice from the outset. Given that we know that the beginning of a teaching career can be a most challenging time (Keogh et al., 2012; Marshall et al., 1990), it is necessary to ensure that beginning teachers are as well-equipped as possible to make the transition to the world of work in a successful way.

Daisy drew comparisons between her university studies and the reality of her work context, indicating that having a process like the model of

DOI: 10.1057/9781137473028.0008

critical reflection had given her a framework that allowed her to 'know what to do when she doesn't know what to do'. In this way, she contributed her survival of the initial transition period to the use of the model:

> Due to feeling so pressured and stressed to exceed the expectations of our school leaders I always felt that Uni practical experiences and some tutorials, lectures, etcetera, didn't set me up for what I was in for. I therefore feel that the model of critical reflection has been the one thing that I was taught at University that was actually useful in my teaching. (Daisy)

Similarly, Kitt explained that constant exposure to the structured model of critical reflection had become instinctual and that she often used the model unconsciously:

> Absolutely. The model of critical reflection becomes so unconscious, that at times you don't realise you have completed it until after. (Kitt)

While it may be an explicit demand for teachers to engage collaboratively with others to reflect on practice, it is often the case that teachers are expected to do so without being given explicit instruction or without being supported to adopt an effective process for undertaking this endeavour effectively. Working with illustrations from the three novice teachers' narratives, it is abundantly clear that they believe this to be the case. The expectation for critical reflection is clearly articulated; yet no particular tools for doing so are advised. The following example illustrates this point:

> Often administration staff expect you to reflect on your teaching but don't give you the tools to do it. I'm lucky enough that I had this embedded in my learning whilst at Uni so that it is a tool that I can use to review my teaching practices. (Daisy)

Extending upon Walkington's (2005) claims that reflective practice be promoted as crucial and that its development is the responsibility of all teacher educators, both at university and within schools, we posit that in fact it is the criticality of such reflection that should be the essential focus of professional interactions across all practice contexts. It is essential to move beyond heavily content-laden professional development programs to support teachers' transitions to the world of work. We argue that, while the programs that are structured around the model of critical reflection are voluntary and therefore do not necessarily involve all students within a particular cohort, it is imperative that that there is a consistent framework within initial teacher education to support a structured approach to critical reflection. Such a framework should permeate all

DOI: 10.1057/9781137473028.0008

content and pedagogy coursework. Strong connections need to be made systematically within the world of work for teachers too, thus reinforcing professional learning according to individual needs, rather than simply focusing on organisational imperatives.

From their commencement in the workplace, beginning teachers almost have the same responsibilities as teachers with many years of experience (Keogh et al., 2012). That is, induction usually sits outside of their classroom responsibilities of developing and delivering the curriculum and managing a full student cohort. In fact, for the novice teacher, induction can be seen as an additional responsibility to juggle multiple demands and responsibilities; hence the references to a profession that 'eats its young' (Halford, 1998, p. 33), takes a 'Robinson Crusoe approach' (Lortie, 1966), and applies a 'sink or swim mentality' (Maciejewski, 2007). Even the very determined novice teacher can find initial transition challenging, as illustrated by Daisy:

> I found it very difficult settling in to a new school, which was very structured and had such high expectations for its staff. I felt I was never good enough and constantly had to reflect on what I was doing to be good enough for what was expected of me. (Daisy)

Apart from being extremely hectic, the first year of teaching for Daisy, Kitt and Poppy was challenging in many ways. As beginning teachers, they seemed to spend a disproportionate amount of time and effort simply keeping their heads above water. The data from each of the teachers indicated a sense of pressure to perform. For example:

> Every term as part of our 'data talks' with the principal we have to reflect on our teaching and student results. If it wasn't for the model of critical reflection I would not have a framework to follow, to realistically reflect on my practice in partnership with my principal...I still engage with the model of critical reflection regularly. After leaving uni it was something that was in-built and I did all the time. It also helped having it in that the context that I was teaching in, as I was forced to reflect on my practice to keep my boss happy and my students moving in their development. (Daisy)

Le Maistre and Paré (2010) suggested that the ability to 'satisfice' – that is, to develop solutions that are sufficient and temporary – enables teachers to survive their first years of practice. However, they also explained that it appears that satisficing is one of the skills that develop with experience. In the data presented, the three novice teachers credit engagement in professional learning and induction programs, such as Education

DOI: 10.1057/9781137473028.0008

Commons and Education Commons International, as having enabled such dispositions to develop early. For example:

> I have used the model of critical reflection on both a positive note and a negative. ... I find the model of critical reflection on positive experiences allows my confidence and self-esteem to grow and gives me that gentle reminder that 'I love this job' and I actually know what I am doing. (Kitt)

In fact, the novice teachers recognised early on that, in order to move beyond mere survival and to thrive in their school contexts, developing effective relationships for professional learning was key. They identified that experienced teachers and administrators have learned how to cope. Through engaging positively with some of their more experienced colleagues, the novice teachers were supported to deal with the complex problems of their initial practice. Given the period of time that had passed for each of them (over two years), they had become resilient, self-efficacious and able to deal with challenges in their classrooms.

Using critical reflection to improve practice and to become a professional

Attempts to improve the status and standing of teachers and teaching are presented in the literature in a range of ways (Frelin, 2013). Professionalisation (often related to the status and standards of the profession overall) (Englund, 1996; Tuinamuana, 2011), professionalism (often focused on the improvement of quality and standards of practice for individual teachers) (Loughran, 2010; Tuinamuana, 2011), and professionality (generally understood as taking up the characteristics of 'good' professional practice) (Frelin, 2013) are sometimes seen as complementary and at other times as contradictory (Hargreaves, 2000). Without going into the argument of which term is best, we suggest that the contradictions inherent in discussions about what constitutes best teaching and practice can be a challenge for individual teachers, especially those new to the profession; hence our advocacy for 'critical reflection in collaboration' as an effective way of establishing shared language and building professional efficacy. This is played out across the novice teachers' responses. For example:

> I use the model of critical reflection both in collaboration and independently. I feel that sometimes the model of critical reflection warrants two heads instead of one. (Kitt)

DOI: 10.1057/9781137473028.0008

As much as it's important for our students to reach their goals, it is the teacher's responsibility to reflect on the distance travelled from pre-assessment to post-assessment for each student. The model of critical reflection has enabled me to do this and constantly improve my teaching and feel confident to try new strategies or see things in a different perspective. (Daisy)

Hargreaves (2000) pointed out that if teachers were asked what it means to *be professional* they usually refer to two things. They sometimes talk about *being professional*, in terms of the quality of what they do and the standards that measure their achievements, and they sometimes talk about *being a professional*, which is usually associated with teachers' perceptions of how they are viewed by others. It is from these perspectives that critical reflection in collaboration with others can impact positively on personal and professional efficacy, providing opportunities to explore what it means to be professional and providing the means to examine the work that is being done from multiple perspectives. This can lead to a consideration of what it means to be a professional in the teaching field more broadly. Teachers are challenged to look beyond their immediate practice and to explore broader curriculum and pedagogical issues that affect the field of education. Such considerations are part of developing professional identity and valuing the professional self (Davey, 2013).

In Poppy's case, becoming a kindy teacher in a distance education context challenged her to re-imagine her practice and her notions of what it means in terms of being a professional in an unfamiliar context. For example:

I believe as a teacher you are always learning. I think when you reflect you are able to see whether a process or idea is working or not. Theorising and thinking otherwise helps me to think about my context and how to make something more user-effective. For example last year I had trouble getting families to send me feedback on their child's learning so I have developed a new way for families to send me feedback. When doing this I had to think about it being user-friendly for parents (easy to use and understand, keeping in mind that they are parents not trained teachers), very clear expectations, and making sure it won't take parents too long to do (as the parents are often time poor). During the term/semester I will reflect on how my new system is working and encourage families to give me feedback as well. (Poppy)

Poppy has been able to adapt her preconceived ways of working to being able to practice effectively in an unfamiliar context. She has constantly challenged herself to view her practice from the perspective of others and to connect her philosophy of early childhood education with practice in

DOI: 10.1057/9781137473028.0008

a distance and online mode of teaching and learning. Her use of critical reflection has enabled her to re-evaluate her notions of what it means to be a professional and to act professionally.

Using critical reflection to support collective action

Broadly speaking, multiple and complex social changes place high demands on teachers – novice or experienced – as do changes to the expectations of schools and school systems as to what teachers should, and will, do. It is our view that responding effectively in educational contexts requires a well-educated, flexible, adaptive and highly competent workforce. With the uptake of high stakes performance outcomes and the introduction of mandatory standards and accreditation regimes (Klenowski & Wyatt-Smith, 2012), teachers are pressured to perform in ways that are responsive to the individual educational needs of the children they teach, at the same time as meeting the demands of society and school systems. The homogenisation of education seems to be at odds with individualised discourses and thus tensions arise (Lingard & Rizvi, 1998; Veloso & Estevinha, 2013).

However, from our examination of the data from Daisy, Kitt and Poppy, we see that they are aware of the pressures of performativity, but they continue to explore ways of privileging the individualisation agenda in collaboration with other teachers and school leaders. For example, Kitt highlighted that:

> The model of critical reflection allows a school/team to come together as a collective to tackle large issues from a school level and has provided me and my school with success. (Kitt)

It is well documented that novice teachers often become discouraged in the pursuit of their career goals and are likely to experience heightened levels of stress and feelings of hopelessness, whereby they question their career choices (Constantine, Wilton, & Caldwell, 2003; Noble, 2009; Rice, Leever, Christopher, & Porter, 2006). The same can be said of more experienced teachers when they are faced with new or unfamiliar situations. Such perceptions can interfere with successful transition in the world of work where unpredictable and rapid changes are evident (Savickas, 1995), where personal demands and expectations in terms of self-determination are great (Deci & Ryan, 2008; Watts, 1996, 2006), and where meeting expectations for agency, adaptability and flexibility are ongoing challenges – and all of that while ensuring that core identity is not compromised (Blustein, 2011).

DOI: 10.1057/9781137473028.0008

However, it is clear from the data presented in this chapter, as well as across the preceding chapters, that teachers involved in the teaching–learning projects and the associated design-based research have used the model of critical reflection to successfully navigating such cross roads (Blustein, 2011). As a result, they have been able to position themselves as successful, lifelong and life-wide learners. As novice teachers, Daisy, Kitt and Poppy enabled themselves within the constraints, or as we like to say, they realised that 'they know what to do when they don't know what to do'. They also explained how they encouraged others in their practice contexts to do likewise, thus supporting collective endeavour and collaborative action.

Conclusion

Novice teachers' attrition and intention to leave the profession continue to be problematic. Indeed, this phenomenon is often attributed to the level and quality of support they receive in their transition to the world of work (Joiner & Edwards, 2008; Noble, 2009). The induction to the profession provided by projects such as Education Commons and Education Commons International seem to have helped the novice teachers, whose voices are heard in this chapter, to align continuing professional development and learning opportunities that meet their immediate needs. Their use of the model of critical reflection seems to have provided them with a way of unpacking what is happening in their classrooms and to reconstruct other ways of being, doing and knowing teaching. As Daisy, Kitt and Poppy have shown, transition to the world of work is enhanced when:

- ▶ a model of critical reflection complements more formal induction processes;
- ▶ effective collaborative relationships are built, thus helping to decrease isolation, intention to leave the profession, and burnout and stress;
- ▶ increased confidence, self-efficacy and positive dispositions are privileged.

Therefore, a holistic approach to supporting novice teacher transition and induction is strongly advocated. This approach should be inclusive, responsive and able to be tailored to suit individual needs, thus promoting

DOI: 10.1057/9781137473028.0008

personal and professional efficacy. It is from this basis that the teaching profession, as a collective, can make informed judgements on the externally imposed performativity regimes governing the profession and the professionals within. Our research suggests that it is through engagement with a model of critical reflection in collaboration that it is possible to re-examine current accountability regimes and guide future professional growth. The expertise of the teacher must be central to the formulation of effective continuing professional learning and development.

DOI: 10.1057/9781137473028.0008

6
Building Workforce Capacity Collaboratively

Abstract: *This chapter presents a framework for a pedagogy of induction based on seven years of design-based research. It suggests a new model of collaborative, critical reflection as a tool for professional learning and induction. The framework of a pedagogy of induction promotes awareness of professional learning from the commencement of university study and continuing across a career. A pedagogy of induction privileges the development of personal and professional agency through collaborative endeavour to build workforce capacity.*

Keywords: career optimism; collaborative critical reflection; pedagogy of induction; professional induction; professional learning; workforce capacity

Henderson, Robyn and Karen Noble. *Professional Learning, Induction and Critical Reflection: Building Workforce Capacity in Education.* Basingstoke: Palgrave Macmillan, 2015. DOI: 10.1057/9781137473028.0009.

DOI: 10.1057/9781137473028.0009

Introduction

Our research into an integrated approach to professional learning, support and induction demonstrates long-term benefits, connecting participants to the discipline of Education and enhancing workforce capacity. This chapter draws together the findings of the analyses presented in the previous chapters, to discuss the types of spaces we need to create to make it possible for the teaching profession to continue to learn.

A synthesis of the outcomes and our learnings from engagement across each of the projects has enabled us to decant a framework for a pedagogy of induction. From the outset, as researchers and authors, our mission has been to re-examine and re-imagine the learning journey of becoming and being a teacher and undertaking the work of teaching. Just as novice teachers are expected to draw together all of their learning from their initial teacher education – to satisfactorily integrate their knowledge from across coursework and practical experiences, thereby learning to be, know and do teacher and teaching – we as researchers will endeavour to do likewise. We will illustrate connectivity across each of the chapters in the book and [re]present a pedagogy of induction that integrates our learning from the various teaching–learning projects that were addressed as part of a design-based research approach.

Each of the chapters addressed aspects of the story behind our push for induction, professional learning and critical reflection as part of learning to 'be' a professional educator. Over time, our learning morphed as we implemented a design-based research approach and extended into new contexts. Chapter 1 introduced the research design and mapped the five teaching–learning projects that contributed to a pedagogy of induction. Chapter 2 explained the foundational understandings of a pedagogy of induction and unpacked the model of critical reflection. The model was used as a way of interrogating teaching and teaching practice within the projects and as a research tool, as well as informing our framing of Chapters 3, 4 and 5. These chapters illustrated the stages of critical reflection: deconstruct and confront, theorise, and think otherwise. Data in each of these chapters highlighted the application of the model in, on and through the research action that contributed to the conceptualisation of a pedagogy of induction.

DOI: 10.1057/9781137473028.0009

Reconceptualising the model of critical reflection

As stated in Chapter 2, we regard critical reflection as a tool that can facilitate learning at the nexus of theory and practice, thereby enabling considerations of theory to inform practice and considerations of practice to inform understandings about theory. Through using the model to provide a structure for each of our teaching–learning projects and as a tool in design-based research, we have generated new understandings about the model of critical reflection and have reconsidered its stages.

We now understand the process of confronting as a useful first stage in undertaking collaborative critical reflection. If a model of critical reflection is to be used to make sense of big picture professional issues, then the processes of identifying and confronting issues seem to be the first step, before attempting to implement the other stages: deconstructing implications for practice, finding ways to traverse the theory practice nexus, and ensuring that future practice is informed by multiple perspectives. The privileging of multiple perspectives is best realised through collaboration, whereby inputs from others can be used to enhance learning.

Therefore, we suggest a new model, a Model of Collaborative Critical Reflection, MOCCR for short, as a noteworthy tool for professional learning and induction. In this model, the essential stages flow as follows:

▸ confront in collaboration;
▸ deconstruct in collaboration;
▸ theorise from multiple perspectives;
▸ think otherwise about practice.

A framework for a pedagogy of induction

The key tenets that prompted the development of a pedagogy of induction can now be realised as a framework to inform effective professional learning and induction across contexts to build workforce capacity. The framework of a pedagogy of induction should:

▸ build on learners' strengths;
▸ understand induction as learning a new Discourse and adopting a new identity;
▸ incorporate collaborative spaces and places for focused teacher talk that is framed by critical reflection;

DOI: 10.1057/9781137473028.0009

▶ ensure professional learning is life-wide and lifelong;
▶ privilege engagement through process as well as content;
▶ promote choice and recognise concomitant rights and responsibilities.

When conceptualised through place and space constructs, professional induction:

▶ privileges belonging;
▶ encourages the sharing of knowledge, skills and experiences;
▶ provides a way of 'knowing what to do when you don't know what to do';
▶ supports informal learning through a focused procedural structure;
▶ privileges real and imagined spaces of teaching as reflection;
▶ highlights individual and collective responsibility for building effective professional learning;
▶ provides opportunities to re-imagine and reshape professional identities to build agency and efficacy;
▶ questions taken-for-granted grand narratives and assumed truths, presenting instead the notion of practice underpinned by multiple theories and perspectives;
▶ ensures personally and professionally meaningful outcomes.

A pedagogy of induction should incorporate:

▶ an awareness of the inter-relatedness of learning needs, interests and abilities with ongoing professional learning;
▶ processes that guide learning, rather than content alone;
▶ learning outside traditional structures and approaches;
▶ the teaching of career optimism.

Engaging pre-service educators in induction to the profession from the outset offers the potential to retain early career educators in the profession, by enabling them to see and understand themselves as teachers and to think like teachers well before they move into the education workforce.

Moving beyond teacher education

A pedagogy of induction will build workforce capacity and is transferable beyond teacher education. Regardless of context or profession, the

DOI: 10.1057/9781137473028.0009

ability to reflect on practice, to identify potential solutions to professional problems or issues, and to be able to adapt, refine and rethink practice is essential. Such an approach can help to ensure that learning is able to continue as new situations and contexts are encountered and can facilitate the transfer of learning from one situation and context to another. A pedagogy of induction offers insights into professional discourses and the potential for problem-solving professional issues at all career stages.

Conclusion

Our research and the development of a pedagogy of induction highlighted induction and professional learning as non-linear and complementary to more traditional approaches. The research project demonstrated that a pedagogy of induction is a creative and integrated approach to professional learning and reminded us that creating new possibilities for learners and learning is an organic process that continues at all career stages. The model of collaborative critical reflection offers a useful tool to enable professionals to work out what they might do when they don't know what to do within a supportive context. It privileges nurturing interactions and relationships with other professionals through shared language and the recognition of individual as well as collective agency.

DOI: 10.1057/9781137473028.0009

References

Allard, A. C., Mayer, D., & Moss, J. (2014). Authentically assessing graduate teaching: Outside and beyond neo-liberal constructs. *Australian Educational Researcher, 41*, 425–443.

Alsup, J. (2006). *Teacher identity discourses: Negotiating personal and professional spaces.* Mahwah, NJ: Lawrence Erlbaum.

Australian Institute for Teaching and School Leadership. (2011). National professional standards for teachers. Retrieved from http://www.teacherstandards.aitsl.edu.au/Static/docs/aitsl_national_professional_standards_for_teachers_240611.pdf.

Ball, D. L., & Cohen, D. K. (1999). Developing practice, developing practitioners: Towards a practice-based theory of professional education. In L. Darling-Hammond & G. Sykes (Eds), *Teaching as the learning profession: Handbook of policy and practice* (pp. 3–32). San Francisco, CA: Jossey-Bass.

Barab, S., & Squire, K. (2004). Design-based research: Putting a stake in the ground. *The Journal of the Learning Sciences, 13*(1), 1–14.

Bartholomaeus, P. (2013). Place-based education and the Australian Curriculum. *Literacy Learning: The Middle Years, 21*(3), 17–23.

Bay, U., & Macfarlane, S. (2011). Teaching critical reflection: A tool for transformative learning in social work? *Social Work Education, 30*(7), 745–758.

Beauchamp, C., & Thomas, L. (2009). Understanding teacher identity: An overview of issues in the literature and implications for teacher education. *Cambridge Journal of Education, 39*(2), 175–189.

Beijaard, D., Meijer, P. C., & Verloop, N. (2004). Reconsidering research on teachers' professional identity. *Teaching and Teacher Education, 20,* 107–128.

Blustein, D. L. (2011). A relational theory of working. *Journal of Voccational Behavior, 79,* 1–17.

Boud, D., & Walker, D. (1998). Promoting reflection in professional courses: The challenge of context. *Studies in Higher Education, 23*(2), 191–206.

Brookfield, S. (1995). *Becoming a critically reflective teacher.* San Francisco, CA: Jossey-Bass.

Buchberger, F., Campos, B. P., Kallos, D., & Stephenson, J. (2001). *Green paper on teacher education in Europe.* Umea, Sweden: Umea University.

Calderhead, J., & Shorrock, S. B. (1997). *Understanding teacher education: Case studies in the professional development of beginning teachers.* London: Falmer Press.

Carver, C., & Scheier, M. (2014). Dispositional optimism. *Trends in Cognitive Sciences, 18,* 293–299.

Choi, T. H. (2013). Autobiographical reflections for teacher professional learning. *Professional Development in Education, 39*(5), 822–840.

Chong, S., Low, E. L., & Goh, K. C. (2011). Emerging professional teacher identity of pre-service teachers. *Australian Journal of Teacher Education, 36*(8), Article 4.

Chouliaraki, L., & Fairclough, N. (1999). *Discourse in late modernity: Rethinking critical discourse analysis.* Edinburgh: Edinburgh University Press.

Clandinin, D. J., & Connelly, F. M. (1996). Teachers' professional knowledge landscapes: Teachers' stories, stories of teachers. School stories, stories of schools. *Educational Researcher, 25*(3), 24–30.

Colbert, J. A., & Wolfe, D. E. (1992). Surviving in urban schools: A collaborative model for a beginning teacher support system. *Journal of Teacher Education, 43*(3), 193–199.

Constantine, M. G., Wilton, L., & Caldwell, L. D. (2003). The role of social support in moderating the relationship between psychological distress and willingness to seek psychological help among Black and Latino college students. *Journal of College Counseling, 6,* 155–165.

Costa, P., & McCrae, R. (1992). *Revised NEO Personality Inventory (NEO-PI-R) and NEO Five-Factor Inventory (NEO-FFI) professional manual.* Odessa, FL: Psychological Assessment Resources.

DOI: 10.1057/9781137473028.0010

Darling-Hammond, L. (2000). Teacher quality and student achievement: A review of state policy evidence. *Education Policy Analysis Archives, 8*(1), 1–44.

Darling-Hammond, L. (2003). Access to quality teaching: An analysis of inequality in California's public schools. *Santa Clara Law Review, 43,* 101–239.

Davey, R. (2013). *The professional identity of teacher educators: Career on the cusp?* London: Routledge.

Deci, E. L., & Ryan, R. M. (2008). Facilitating optimal motivation and psychological well-being across life's domains. *Canadian Psychology, 49,* 14–23.

Dewey, J. (1933). *How we think.* Boston, MA: Heath.

Edwards, R., Ranson, S., & Strain, M. (2002). Reflexivity: Towards a theory of lifelong learning. *International Journal of Lifelong Learning, 21*(6), 525–536.

Englund, T. (1996). Are professional teachers a good thing? In I. Goodson & A. Hargreaves (Eds), *Teachers' professional lives.* London: Falmer.

Ewing, R., & Manuel, J. (2005). Retaining quality early career teachers in the profession: New teacher narratives. *Change: Transformations in Education, 8*(1), 1–16.

Fairclough, N. (2001). *Language and power* (2nd ed.). London: Longman.

Falabella, A. (2014). The performing school: The effects of market and accountability policies. *Education Policy Analysis Archives, 22*(70), 1–26.

Fantilli, R., & McDougall, D. E. (2009). A study of novice teachers: Challenges and supports in the first years. *Teaching and Teacher Education, 25*(6), 825–841.

Feinberg, J. (2013). Wordle™ [Website]. Retrieved from http://www.wordle.net/.

Flores, M. A., & Day, C. (2006). Contexts which shape and reshape new teachers' identities: A multi-perspective study. *Teaching and Teacher Education, 22,* 219–232.

Frelin, A. (2013). *Exploring relational professionalism in schools.* Rotterdam, The Netherlands: Sense.

Gee, J. P. (1996). *Social linguistics and literacies: Ideology in discourses* (2nd ed.). London: Falmer Press.

Gee, J. P. (2004). *Situated language and learning: A critique of traditional school.* New York, NY: Routledge.

DOI: 10.1057/9781137473028.0010

Gee, J. P. (2014). Language as saying, doing and being. In J. Angermuller, D. Maingueneau & R. Wodak (Eds), *The discourse studies reader: Main currents in theory and analysis* (pp. 234–243). Philadelphia, PA: John Benjamin.

Gonzales, N., Moll, L. C., & Amanti, C. (2005a). Introduction: Theorizing practices. In N. Gonzales, L. C. Moll & C. Amanti (Eds), *Funds of knowledge: Theorizing practices in households, communities, and classrooms* (pp. 1–24). NewYork, NY: Routledge.

Gonzales, N., Moll, L. C., & Amanti, C. (Eds) (2005b). *Funds of knowledge: Theorizing practices in households, communities, and classrooms*. New York: Routledge.

Gruenewald, D. (2003). Foundations of place: A multidisciplinary framework for place-conscious education. *American Educational Research Journal, 40*(3), 619–654.

Gur-Ze'ev, I., Masschelein, J., & Blake, N. (2001). Reflectivity, reflection, and counter-education. *Studies in Philosophy and Education, 20*(2), 93–106.

Halford, J. (1998). Easing the way for new teachers. *Educational Leadership, 55*(5), 33–36.

Hardy, I. (2013). Testing that counts: Contesting national literacy assessment policy in complex schooling settings. *Australian Journal of Language and Literacy, 36*(2), 67–77.

Hargreaves, A. (1994). *Changing teachers, changing times: Teachers' work and culture in the postmodern age*. New York, NY: Teachers College Press.

Hargreaves, A. (2000). Four ages of professionalism and professional learning. *Teachers and Teaching: Theory and Practice, 6*(2), 151–182.

Harvey, D. (1996). *Justice, nature and the geography of difference*. Cambridge, MA: Blackwell.

Henderson, R. (2004). Recognising difference: One of the challenges of using a multiliteracies approach? *Practically Primary, 9*(2), 11–14.

Henderson, R. (2012). Teaching literacies: Pedagogical possibilities. In R. Henderson (Ed.), *Teaching literacies in the middle years: Pedagogies and diversity* (pp. 269–278). South Melbourne, Vic.: Oxford University Press.

Henderson, R., Abawi, L., & Conway, J. (2011). Exposing threads: Creating connections in teaching and learning. In L. Abawi, J. Conway, & R. Henderson (Eds), *Creating connections in teaching and learning* (pp. 1–14). Charlotte, NC: Information Age Publishing.

DOI: 10.1057/9781137473028.0010

Henderson, R., & Hirst, E. (2007). Reframing academic literacy: Re-examining a short-course for 'disadvantaged' tertiary students. *English Teaching: Practice and Critique, 6*(2), 25–38.

Henderson, R., & Lennon, S. (2014). A conversation about research as risky business: Making visible the invisible in rural research locations. In S. White & M. Corbett (Eds), *Doing educational research in rural settings: Methodological issues, international perspectives and practical solutions* (pp. 119–134). London: Routledge.

Henderson, R., & Noble, K. (2009). FYI (First Year Infusion): A vaccine for the first year plague in a regional university. In C. Boylan (Ed.), *Proceedings of the 25th National Rural Education Conference: Education in a Digital Present: Enriching Rural Communities* (pp. 85–93). Adelaide, SA: Society for the Provision of Education in Rural Australia.

Henderson, R., & Noble, K. (2013). Thinking about first year retention in teacher education: Three students in a regional university and their metaphors of survival. *Australian and International Journal of Rural Education, 23*(2), 65–75.

Henderson, R., Noble, K., & Cross, K. (2013). Additional Professional Induction Strategy (APIS): Education Commons, a strategy to support transition to the world of work. *Australian and International Journal of Rural Education, 23*(1), 61–74.

Henderson, R., Noble, K., & De George-Walker, L. (2009). Transitioning into university: 'Interrupted' first year students problem-solving their way into study. *Studies in Learning, Evaluation, Innovation and Development, 6*(1), 51–64.

Hickson, H. (2011). Critical reflection: Reflecting on learning to be reflective. *Reflective Practice: International and multidisciplinary perspectives, 12*(6), 829–939.

Hollins, E. R. (2011). Teacher preparation for quality teaching. *Journal of Teacher Education, 62*(4), 395–407.

Holloway, L., & Hubbard, P. (2001). *People and place: The extraordinary geographies of everyday life.* New York, NY: Routledge.

Joiner, S., & Edwards, J. (2008). Novice teachers: Where are they going and why don't they stay? *Journal of Cross-Disciplinary Perspectives in Education, 1*(1), 36–43.

Kalantzis, M., & Cope, B. (n.d.). Repertoires of practice. Retrieved from http://newlearningonline.com/learning-by-design/glossary/repertoire-of-practice.

DOI: 10.1057/9781137473028.0010

Kalantzis, M., Cope, B., & the Learning by Design Project Group (2005). *Learning by design*. Melbourne, Vic.: Victorian Schools Innovation Commission & Common Ground Publishing.

Keogh, J., Garvis, S., Pendergast, D., & Diamond, P. (2012). Self-determination: Using agency, efficacy and resilience (AER) to counter novice teachers' experiences of intensification. *Australian Journal of Teacher Education, 37*(8), 46–65.

Klenowski, V., & Wyatt-Smith, C. (2012). The impact of high stakes testing: The Australian story. *Assessment in Education: Principles, Policy and Practice, 19*(1), 65–79. doi: 10.1080/0969594X.2011.592972.

Kocatepe, M. (2004). Personal reflections on the ESL label and virtual schoolbags. *Practically Primary, 9*(3), 18.

Kuusisaari, H. (2013). Teachers' collaborative learning: Development of teaching in group discussions. *Teachers and Teaching: Theory and Practice, 19*(1), 50–62.

Lampert, M. (1985). How do teachers manage to teach? Perspectives on problems in practice. *Harvard Educational Review, 55*(2), 178–194.

Lather, P., & Smithies, C. (1997). *Troubling the angels: Women living with HIV/aids*. Boulder, CO: Westview Press.

Lave, J., & Wenger, E. (1999). Learning and pedagogies in communities of practice. In J. Leach & B. Moon (Eds), *Learners and pedagogy* (pp. 21–33). London: Paul Chapman Publishing.

Le Maistre, C., & Paré, A. (2010). Whatever it takes: How beginning teachers learn to survive. *Teaching and Teacher Education, 26*(3), 559–564.

Lehtovuori, P. (2005). *Experience and conflict: The dialectics of the production of public urban space in the light of new event venues in Helsinki 1993–2003*. (Doctor of Philosophy), Helsinki University of Technoloogy, Espoo, Finland.

Lingard, B., & Rizvi, F. (1998). Globalisation and the fear of homogenisation in education. *Change: Transformations in Education, 1*(1), 62–71.

Lortie, D. C. (1966). *Teacher socialization: The Robinson Crusoe model. In the real world of the beginning teacher*. Washington, DC: National Commission on Teacher Education and Professional Standards (ERIC Document Reproduction Service No. ED03061).

Loughran, J. (2002). Effective reflective practice: In search of meaning in learning about teaching. *Journal of Teacher Education, 53*(1), 33–43.

DOI: 10.1057/9781137473028.0010

Loughran, J. (2006). A response to 'Reflecting on the self'. *Reflective Practice, 7*(1), 43–53.

Loughran, J. (2007). Enacting a pedagogy of teacher education. In T. Russell & J. Loughran (Eds), *Enacting a pedagogy of teacher education: Values, relationships and practice* (pp. 1–15). London: Routledge.

Loughran, J. (2010). Seeking knowledge for teaching teaching: Moving beyond stories. *Studying Teacher Education, 6*(3), 221–226.

Lovett, S., & Gilmore, A. (2003). Teachers' learning journeys: The quality learning circle as a model of professional development. *School Effectiveness and School Improvement: An International Journal of Research, Policy and Practice, 14*(2), 189–211.

Lowenthal, D. (1961). Geography, experience and imagination: Towards a geographical epistemology. *Annals of the American Association of Geographers, 51*(3), 241–260.

Luthans, F. (2002). The need for and meaning of positive organizational behavior. *Journal of Organizational Behavior, 23*, 695–706.

Luthans, F., & Youssef, C. M. (2007). Emerging positive organizational behavior. *Journal of Management, 33*, 321–349.

Macfarlane, K., Noble, K., Kilderry, A., & Nolan, A. (2006). Developing skills of thinking otherwise and critical reflection. In K. Noble, K. Macfarlane, & J. Cartmel (Eds), *Circles of change: Challenging orthodoxy in practitioner supervision* (pp. 11–20). Frenchs Forest, NSW: Pearson.

Maciejewski, J. (2007). Supporting new teachers: Are induction programs worth the cost? *District Administration, 43*(9), 48–52.

Marshall, P., Fittinghoff, S., & Cheney, C. O. (1990). Beginning teacher developmental stages: Implications for creating collaborative internship programs. *Teacher Education Quarterly, 17*(3), 25–35.

McIlveen, P., Burton, L. J., & Beccaria, G. (2013). A short form of the Career Futures Inventory. *Journal of Career Assessment, 21*(1), 127–138.

McIlveen, P., & Patton, W. (2007). Narrative career counselling: Theory and exemplars of practice. *Australian Psychologist, 42*(3), 226–235.

McMahon, M., & Patton, W. (1995). Development of a systems theory of career development. *Australian Journal of Career Development, 4*, 15–20.

McNaught, C., & Lam, P. (2010). Using Wordle as a supplementary research tool. *The Qualitative Report, 15*(3), 630–643.

Mills, J. (2001). Self-construction through conversation and narrative in interviews. *Educational Review, 53*(3), 285–301.

DOI: 10.1057/9781137473028.0010

Moll, L. C., Amanti, C., Neff, D., & Gonzales, N. (1992). Funds of knowledge for teaching: Using a qualitative approach to connect homes and classrooms. *Theory into Practice, XXXI*(2), 132–141.

Mortari, L. (2012). Learning thoughtful reflection in teacher education. *Teachers and Teaching: Theory and Practice, 18*(5), 525–545.

Murray, J. (2012). Changing places, changing spaces: Towards understanding teacher education's locations through space-time. *Journal of Education for Teaching, 38*(5), 245–267.

Murray, J. (2014). Teacher educators' constructions of professionalism: Change and diversity in teacher education. *Asia Pacific Journal of Teacher Education, 42*(1), 7–21.

Nicholas, M. (2015). Informed assessment: Self-doubt and reflecting on practice. *Literacy Learning: The Middle Years, 23*(1), 7–13.

Noble, K. (2009). *Understanding workplace bullying in early childhood contexts: Safeguarding the workplace to address burnout and stress.* Saarbrücken, Germany: VDM Verlag Dr Müller.

Noble, K., & Henderson, R. (2008). Engaging with images and stories: Using a Learning Circle approach to develop agency of beginning 'at-risk' pre-service teachers. *Australian Journal of Teacher Education, 33*(1), 1–16.

Noble, K., & Henderson, R. (2012). What is capacity building and why does it matter?: Developing a model of workforce capacity building through the case of Education Commons. In P. A. Danaher, L. De George-Walker, R. Henderson, K. J. Matthews, W. Midgley, K. Noble, M. A. Tyler, & C. Arden (Eds), *Constructing capacities: Building capacity through learning and engagement* (pp. 51–67). Newcastle upon Tyne: Cambridge Scholars Publishing.

Noble, K., Macfarlane, K., & Cartmel, J. (Eds) (2006). *Circles of change: Challenging orthodoxy in practitioner supervision.* Frenchs Forest, NSW: Pearson.

Noble, K., & McIlveen, P. (2012). Being, knowing, and doing: A model for reflexivity in social constructionist practices. In P. McIlveen & D. E. Schultheiss (Eds), *Social constructionism in vocational psychology and career development* (pp. 105–113). Rotterdam, The Netherlands: Sense.

Noddings, N. (1984). *Caring: A feminine approach to ethics and moral education.* Berkeley, CA: University of California Press.

O'Connell Rust, F. (2009). Teacher research and the problem of practice. *Teachers College Record, 111*(8), 1882–1893.

DOI: 10.1057/9781137473028.0010

Patterson, A. (1997). Critical discourse analysis: A condition of doubt. *Discourse: Studies in the cultural politics of education, 18*(3), 425–435.

Patton, W., & McMahon, M. (1999). *Career development and systems theory: A new relationship*. Pacific Grove, CA: Brooks/Cole.

Patton, W., & McMahon, M. (2006). *Career development and systems theory: Connecting theory and practice*. Rotterdam, The Netherlands: Sense.

Pyne, C. (2014). A quality education begins with the best teachers, says Christopher Pyne [Opinion piece]. Retrieved from http://www. canberratimes.com.au/federal-politics/political-opinion/a-quality-education-begins-with-the-beste-teachers-says-christopher-pyne-20140219-32z61.

Ravensbergen, F., & VanderPlaat, M. (2010). Learning circles: One form of knowledge production in social action research. *McGill Journal of Education, 45*(3), 339–350.

Rice, K. G., Leever, B. A., Christopher, J., & Porter, J. D. (2006). Perfectionism, stress, and social (dis)connection: A short-term study of hopelessness, depression, and academic adjustment among honors students. *Journal of Counseling Psychology, 53*(4), 524–534.

Rottinghaus, P. J., Day, S. X., & Borgen, F. H. (2005). The Career Futures Inventory: A measure of career-related adaptability and optimism. *Journal of Career Assessment, 13*(1), 3–24.

Ryan, M. (2011). Improving reflective writing in higher education: A social semiotic perspective. *Teaching in Higher Education, 16*(1), 99–111.

Ryan, M. (2012). Conceptualising and teaching discursive and performative reflection in higher education. *Studies in Continuing Education, 34*(2), 207–223.

Sachs, J. (2005). Teacher education and the development of professional identity: Learning to be a teacher. In P. Denicolo & M. Kompf (Eds), *Connecting policy and practice: Challenges for teaching and learning in schools and universities* (pp. 5–21). Oxford: Routledge.

Savickas, M. L. (1995). Constructivist counseling for career indecision. *The Career Development Quarterly, 43*(4), 363–373.

Schön, D. (1983). *The reflective practitioner: How professionals think in action*. London: Temple Smith.

Sjølie, E. (2014). The role of theory in teacher education: Reconsidered from a student teacher perspective. *Journal of Curriculum Studies, 46*(6), 729–750.

DOI: 10.1057/9781137473028.0010

Skourdoumbis, A. (2014). International 'benchmarking' studies and the identification of 'education best practice': A focus on classroom teachers and their practices. *Australian Educational Researcher, 41*, 411–423.

Smith, M., & Trede, F. (2013). Reflective practice in the transition phase from university student to novice graduate: Implications for teaching reflective practice. *Higher Education Research and Development, 32*(4), 632–645.

Tam, A. C. F. (2015). The role of a professional learning community in teacher change: A perspective from beliefs and practices. *Teachers and Teaching: Theory and Practice, 21*(1), 22–43.

Temmerman, N., Noble, K., & Danaher, P. A. (2010). Futureproofing faculties of education in Australian regional universities: Three sites of pressure and possibility. *Studies in Learning, Evaluation, Innovation and Development, 7*(2), 1–14.

The Design-Based Research Collective (2003). Design-based research: An emerging paradigm for educational inquiry. *Educational Researcher, 32*(1), 5–8.

Thomas, L., & Beauchamp, C. (2007). Learning to live well as teachers in a changing world: Insights into developing a professional identity in teacher education. *Journal of Educational Thought, 41*(3), 229–243.

Thomson, P. (2002). *Schooling the rustbelt kids: Making the difference in changing times.* Crows Nest, NSW: Allen & Unwin.

Tinto, V. (2008, November 1). *Access without support is not opportunity.* Paper presented at the 36th Annual Institute for Chief Academic Officers, The Council of Independent Colleges, Seattle, Washington.

Tuinamuana, K. (2011). Teacher professional standards, accountability and ideology: Alternative discourses. *Australian Journal of Teacher Education, 36*(12), 72–82.

Van Rensburg, H., Noble, K., & McIlveen, P. (in press). Influencing pre-service teachers' intentions to teach in rural locations. *Australian and International Journal of Rural Education.*

Veloso, L., & Estevinha, S. (2013). Differentiation versus homogenisation of education systems in Europe: Political aims and welfare regimes. *International Journal of Educational Research, 62*, 187–198.

Verstegen, D., & Zhang, Z. (2012). Retaining American K-12 teachers in public education: Findings from an analysis of longitudinal national data using structural equation modeling. *Academic Leadership: The*

DOI: 10.1057/9781137473028.0010

Online Journal, 10(1). Retrieved from http://www.academicleadership. org.

Walkington, J. (2005). Mentoring pre-service teachers in the preschool setting: Perceptions of the role. *Australian Journal of Early Childhood, 30*(1), 28–35.

Wang, F., & Hannafin, M. J. (2005). Design-based research and technology-enhanced learning environments. *Educational Technology Research and Development, 53*(4), 5–23.

Watts, A. G. (1996). Socio-political ideologies in guidance. In A. G. Watts, B. Law, J. Killeen, J. M. Kidd, & R. Hawthorn (Eds), *Rethinking careers education and guidance: Theory, policy and practice* (pp. 351–365). London: Routledge.

Watts, A. G. (2006). *Career development learning and employability.* York, UK: The Higher Education Academy.

Wilson, S. M., Floden, R. E., & Ferrini-Mundy, J. (2001). *Teacher preparation research: Current knowledge, gaps and recommendations.* Seattle, WA: University of Washington, Center for the Study of Teaching and Policy.

Wright, J. K. (1947). Terrae incognitae: The place of imagination in geography. *Annals of the American Association of Geographers, 37*(1), 1–15.

Zeichner, K. (2010). Rethinking the connections between campus courses and field experiences in college- and university-based teacher education. *Journal of Teacher Education, 61*(1–2), 89–99.

Zeichner, K., & Liston, D. P. (1996). *Reflective teaching: An introduction.* Mahwah, NJ: Lawrence Erlbaum Associates.

DOI: 10.1057/9781137473028.0010

Index

DOI: 10.1057/9781137473028.0011

DOI: 10.1057/9781137473028.0011

DOI: 10.1057/9781137473028.0011

DOI: 10.1057/9781137473028.0011

CPSIA information can be obtained at www.ICGtesting.com
Printed in the USA
LVOW11*2042190415

435253LV00001B/2/P